WE ARE
ONE

HUMANITY'S COMMON VALUES

WE ARE ONE

HUMANITY'S COMMON VALUES

BEN ADAM

PARTRIDGE

A Penguin Random House Company

Print information available on the last page.

To order additional copies of this book, contact
Partridge India
000 800 10062 62
orders.india@partridgepublishing.com

www.partridgepublishing.com/india

CONTENTS

Context 1

   Consciousness and the Sanctity of Life 5

   Sow and Reap.. 18

   Compassion..27

   Conviction and Surrender....................................38

   Generosity and Gratitude....................................47

   Delayed Gratification 56

   Labor and Perseverance......................................64

   Meaning to Life 72

   Transcendence and Immanence..............................80

   Moderation and Detachment 88

   Oneness and Interdependence................................98

   Selflessness and Egolessness................................107

   Sharing the Message 116

Way Forward..125

Sources (By Chapter)..129

DEDICATION

This work is dedicated to humanity, humanitarian causes, and our children. It is hoped that this work will help in creating a more peaceful and happier world for them, and for a better life on earth, in general.

CONTEXT

This book is born at a moment in time that augurs monumental change for humanity and the environment. The impact of this change may be cataclysmic. At no point in history has humanity represented such a great threat to itself, and life on Earth as we know it. The means of destruction, in terms of potential impact on life and the environment, have never been greater. They range from human induced climate change to weapons of mass destruction to powerful means of mass communication that are subject to gross manipulation. As, if not more, portentous are the social and economic forces that employ these means to satisfy an incessant drive to accumulate material wealth and influence, as well as to prevail culturally and geo-politically. This state of affairs fuels a dynamic that is very likely to end in multiple calamities; whether on the environmental front (as various tipping points are breached), or through the clash of cultures, sustained with geopolitical, economic, media and military force.

The globe is shrinking by the day, be that through communication media, transportation, impact of climate change, global alliances, or potential impact of industrial and military growth and development. As the globe transforms into a proverbial village, or a perceptually shrinking vehicle carrying us through space, there is a need to appreciate how more intertwined human destiny is, and how we can build on common, or universal, values to achieve a more balanced, inclusive, and sustainable development trajectory towards a shared vision.

This book was inspired by a life long journey I have embarked upon that has taken me from the East to the West, and back again, only to ultimately end up in a common space amidst the globalised world in which we find ourselves. This has been a painful journey. One in which I was rejected in both the Eastern or Western culture/s I was raised in. While my international experience led to marked career success, it was destructive spiritually. The "disconnectedness" and estrangement I felt from society and environment led to workaholism, and other obsessive behavior that almost killed me, and significantly hurt my family. I was ultimately saved by spirituality. Thanks to a loving wife, a loving family, and other kindly souls around me. With this experience I ventured to transmute all the pain and suffering I had gone through, into healing for myself, my family, and humanity's daunting ailments. I reviewed all the world's major social governance systems that had withstood the test of time, geography, and led to sustainable social development and environmental awareness.

The point of departure towards the end of my journey was the identification of a set of universal values shared by major faiths and ideologies prescribing social governance. The problem with religions and ideologies, when they age, is that they are transformed from being a spiritually empowering system of ideals to a construct that is often institutionalized and utilized by vested interests to achieve ends that are not always in line with their original goals and values. The key towards avoiding this outcome is to look beyond the external form to the internal essence and values, and where they originally aimed to guide human society. While some values may change or evolve, there is a common core set that appears to recur time and again.

The ultimate goal of all faiths is the ascent of man, whether spiritually, socially, economically, and/or environmentally. Man and society have reached their most acclaimed heights when they have been most inclusive, inter-connected, synergistically collaborative, knowledge seeking, aware and in harmony with nature. Societies such as those in Mesopotamia, Canaan (Phoenicia), Egypt, Greece, China, India, Andalusia, South America, Europe, North America, and East Asia have taken humanity to new heights when they espoused these values, and generally the opposite when they abandoned them.

In what follows is a concise presentation of the more salient of these universal values seen as essential in decisively realizing the continued ascent of man. While there have been multiple efforts to determine common ground between faiths, there does not appear to have been an initiative to identify such common ground, in terms of a limited number of values, between faiths and non-theistic social governance systems, such as the consensual democracy based values expressed in the UN Universal Declaration of Human Rights and the Ethical Charter of the Socialist International. This work aims to present a highly intuitive booklet that is accessible to a wide audience within the constraint of conserving time and effort for the reader, while still encapsulating a concentrated distillation of the essence of faiths and social governance ideologies, that encompass a very large proportion of the world's population of adherents, followers and proponents. I believe now is a crucial time for world society to arrive at its spiritual common core, and trust this work will help us get there somewhat more quickly. What is at stake is no less than survival of the human species, while paradoxically there has been no time in history when the potential for perceiving our inter-connectedness with each other and mother earth, has been greater.

CONSCIOUSNESS AND THE SANCTITY OF LIFE

(LIVE AND LET LIVE)

Every major religion and social ideology (or governance model) upholds the sanctity of life, in one means or the other. In most of these religions, spiritual traditions or social models, it is not only human life that is considered sacred. All life is recognized as being interdependent, and at the core of these belief systems, the elevation of consciousness (and/or awareness) is how life is propagated, and the ascent of man achieved. What differentiates plant, from animal, from primitive man, from developed man is degree of consciousness and awareness. The ideal state implied by reciprocal consciousness is that human society becomes harmoniously integrated, both within itself, and with the environment around it, in a fashion that propagates life in terms of quality, primarily, and quantity, secondarily. Below are excerpts from referential scriptures and texts supporting this conclusion (the order in which faiths and relevant scriptures are quoted relates, generally, to the author's estimate of *practicing* adherents of the respective faiths, beginning with the Abrahamic, then the Vedic, while closing with the non-theistic social governance systems):

ISLAM

In the name of the Compassionate and the Merciful:

For this reason did We prescribe to the children of Israel that whoever slays a soul, unless it be for manslaughter or for mischief in the land, it is as though he slew all men; and whoever keeps it alive, it is as though he kept alive all men. (Sanctity of Life) **The Quran 5-32.**[1]

"There is reward in [caring for] every living being."(Sanctity of Life)—**The Prophet Mohammed, Sahih Muslim, 7:44**[2]

Allah's Apostle (Mohammed PBUH) said, "A prostitute was forgiven by Allah, because, passing by a panting dog near a well and seeing that the dog was about to die of thirst, she took off her shoe, and tying it with her head-cover she drew out some water for it. So, Allah forgave her because of that." (Sanctity of Life)—**The Prophet Mohammed, Sahih Al-Bukhari**[3]

CHRISTIANITY AND JUDAISM

"You shall not murder" **The Old Testament, Exodus 20:13, World English Bible (WEB), www.biblegateway.com**

"Whoever sheds man's blood, his blood will be shed by man, for God made man in his own image." **The Old Testament, Genesis 9:6. World English Bible (WEB), www.biblegateway.com**

"The heart of the discerning gets knowledge. The ear of the wise seeks knowledge." **The Old Testament, Proverbs 18:15. World English Bible (WEB), www.biblegateway.com**

CHRISTIANITY

For God so loved the world, that he gave his one and only Son, that whoever believes in him should not perish, but have eternal life. **The Bible, John 3:16. World English Bible (WEB), www.biblegateway.com**

Give your servant therefore an understanding heart to judge your people, that I may discern between good and evil; for who is able to judge this great people of yours?" **The Bible, Kings 3:9. World English Bible (WEB), www.biblegateway.com**

JUDAISM

He who destroys one person has dealt a blow at the entire universe, and similarly, he who makes life livable for one person has sustained the whole world. **The Talmud,** *The Wisdom of the Talmud,* **by Ben Zion Bokser, [1951],**[4]

HINDUISM

Do not injure the beings living on the earth, in the air and in the water. **Yajur Veda, 36:18**[5]

Verily the highest virtue of man is sparing the life of others. **Mahabharata 1.11.12, The Mahabharata** *of Krishna-Dwaipayana Vyasa* **translated by Kisari Mohan Ganguli [published between 1883 and 1896], http://www.sacred-texts. com/hin/maha/index.htm**

"Do not harm anything." **Rig Veda, Source: The Hindu history By Akshoy Kumar Mazumdar**[6]

BUDDHISM

One should neither kill nor cause to kill. **Dhammapada 10:129 (Narada Translation, 1959)**

Whoso destroys life, Tells lies, Takes what is not given, commits sexual misconduct, and is addicted to intoxicating drinks—Such a one roots out oneself in this very world. **Dhammapada 18:246, Narada Translation 1959**

TAOISM

Do not kill but always be mindful of the host of living beings. *Scripture on Setting the Will on Wisdom* **(DZ325). Livia Kohn.**[7]

CONFUCIANISM

To love a thing means wanting it to live. **Confucius, *Analects*, 6th century B.C. (12.10, translated by Ch'u Chai and Winberg Chai).**

UNIVERSAL HUMAN RIGHTS

Everyone has the right to *life*, liberty and security of person. **Article (3), UN Universal Declaration of Human Rights, http://www.state.gov/j/drl/rls/irf/2008/108544.htm, (This material is in the public domain and may be reprinted without permission; citation of this source is appreciated.)**

(1) Everyone has the right to education. Education shall be free, at least in the elementary and fundamental stages.

Elementary education shall be compulsory. Technical and professional education shall be made generally available and higher education shall be equally accessible to all on the basis of merit. (2) Education shall be directed to the full development of the human personality and to the strengthening of respect for human rights and fundamental freedoms. It shall *promote understanding,* tolerance and friendship *among all nations, racial or religious groups,* and shall further the activities of the United Nations for the maintenance of peace. **Article (26), UN Universal Declaration of Human Rights, http://www.state. gov/j/drl/rls/irf/2008/108544.htm, (This material is in the public domain and may be reprinted without permission; citation of this source is appreciated.)**

SOCIALISM

To guarantee, under all circumstances, the respect of human dignity and to act in accordance with the Universal Declaration of Human Rights and the other important conventions adopted by the United Nations and its institutions. To ban the death penalty. **ETHICAL CHARTER *of the* SOCIALIST INTERNATIONAL,**[8]

PERSONAL EXPERIENCE

Fear has been a constant companion of mine since childhood. I wasn't sure why. I thought perhaps it had to do with feeling I did not belong, as my family moved from country to country, at least twice to three times by the time I was eight. Perhaps it was their over-protectiveness and my over-sensitivity, or that initially, faith was not a big part of our lives. What I do know is that fear is fuelled by not knowing what to expect, or how to react, when the expected, or unexpected, happens. It is fuelled by feeling vulnerable. This, I believe, is what happens when calm **awareness or consciousness** is lacking. As a child, I was subject to racial and mental abuse. My reaction was to want to block feeling, either though isolation, codependency (dysfunctional relationships), or eventually, substance abuse. I believe that alienation and blocking out feeling (even exposure to real life) through obsessive behavior is a phenomenon that is widespread, and is by no means isolated to cases such as mine, in this day and age. It is only through spiritual growth that I was able to travel from "self-consciousness" to "life consciousness", from inward focus to outward focus, from fear to love, and from delusion to truth. Cherishing life and sanctifying it is not merely by "not killing", but also by being aware of, and consciously, integrating with life around me, instead of obsessing about my own, or so I learned the hard way. As a child in the UK I was subjected to racial slurs like "Paki", "wog", and asked to "go home", even though I was neither Pakistani nor black, it was perhaps because I was of dark complexion. When I finally did go home I was labelled the "English kid" by my compatriots in class because of my broken accent in my own language and proficiency in English. In both cases, my being perceived as "different" whether physically or verbally triggered a sense of distance, callousness, and perhaps fear, in the people around me. There was also cultural baggage and negative social conditioning towards other cultures with which there were past conflicts, that I now realize, had also encouraged such behavior. In both societies there was a demonization of "the other" fuelled by historic conflicts. The lack of awareness or consciousness of the racial bias visited on my colleagues made them oblivious to the humiliation they were subjecting me to. In fact, I actually sensed they saw me as a lower life form than "their kind", and in a state of frenzy, I can see how that visceral conviction could lead to them considering my life less valuable than theirs! Thankfully, while I was beaten up a few times, I was never subjected to mob violence, or explicit threats to my life. We are guided by major faiths to treat fellow humans, animals and plants, with kindness, conscientiousness, and consideration. Time and again ignorance, bigotry, demonizing other cultures, faiths, and races has led to death and destruction. Yet it continues! Perhaps the occasions I felt most welcome was when I visited Scandinavian countries, or was amongst other foreigners volunteering for UN initiatives. Perhaps in the case of the former the lighter cultural baggage (along with more progressive education), and in the latter case, all of us feeling like strangers that needed to console and empathize with each other, are the factors that fed this sense of comfort, familiarity, or belonging.

I still feel that I carry bias against other cultures from my early experiences, and I consciously work on letting go of resentments on a daily basis. What works for me is meditating on awareness of what is around me, including meditating on others' feelings and needs. That consciousness is what keeps respect for life awake in me, and realize that what has befallen me is a result of a cycle of resentment that must be broken, in order for it to stop.

The progress of life is enriched by synergistically engaging with the differences of what different cultures, and even different life forms, have to offer each other. Still, nurturing this attitude takes daily practice, I have found, or I can easily regress towards resentment and isolation. I must constantly be aware of how my talents, strengths or what I have to offer can enrich life for everyone, as opposed to what I expect everyone to do to meet my wants and grievances.

CONCLUDING REMARKS

Warfare in the 20th century was responsible for over 150 million deaths (mainly due to two world wars emanating from the West, and internal conflicts in China and the Soviet Union). Yet these very powers are entrusted by humanity to safeguard the world through the UN Security Council?! Interestingly it is the more "advanced" countries that were responsible for the bulk of deaths in the 20th century. The only clearly common feature of all permanent Security Council members is military might, and the power to annihilate life en masse through nuclear and other means (economic might has only become a common feature of all these members relatively recently). What kind of a message does that send to countries and governments that aspire to "greatness"! Does it not imply that a society or country is only likely to safeguard its destiny and have a serious impact on world affairs if it acquires the means to kill en masse, or deter from killing en masse?! Does this not imply that the "law of the jungle" continues to prevail. With the spread of high tech weapons, a world war in the 21st century would potentially be much more destructive, especially if fortified by vilification and de-humanization of "the other", and the continuation of a "might is right" paradigm in world affairs. A paradigm that renders international forums for justice like the International Criminal Court (ICC) or the International Court of Justice (ICJ) ineffective vis-à-vis powerful states.

In the 21st century we are vulnerable to as large a scale of destruction visited by environmental instability, as in wars, unless immediate evasive steps are taken. Lack of consciousness and awareness underlie wars, and the insensitivity towards the environment, in the pursuit of material gain. There are no victors when one fights life, and consciousness (or awareness, knowledge, truth, learning and understanding). In fact the very nature or definition of life is based on awareness or consciousness, interaction and constructive response to perceived stimuli. From **consciousness** springs perception of **faith, truth, and love (or compassion)**. All the other universal values are based on or related to these three precepts, which emanate from their common source (of consciousness).

An outsider looking upon the Earth during the 20th, and early 21st century, given world wars, the assault on the environment and cultural intolerance would not unreasonably conclude that humanity's was a "Live and Let Die" culture, as opposed to the "Live and Let Live" value that cuts across all major spiritual traditions.

YOUR VIEWS AND REFLECTIONS

CHAPTER 1 (CONSCIOUSNESS AND SACTITY OF LIFE)

How does Consciousness/Awareness relate to Life, and its Sanctity, in your mind? Do you value Consciousness? How important is all Life around you to your own?

_____

_____

Does caring for Life around you enrich yours? How?

_____

_____

_____

How important is caring for the environment to your life? How does war impact upon the quality of your life?

_____

_____

How important is knowledge, including knowledge of "the other" different cultures, and different life forms to your life?

_____

_____

How does fear, and disconnectedness impact on the quality of your Life, and the lives of those around you? How can awareness address those fears, and improve your life?

_____

_____

What action/s do you intend to take to expand consciousness and awareness of Life around you? When? What is/are your priority/ies?

_____

_____

_____

Do you hold resentments of those around you? Of the hand you have been dealt? How can these be constructively resolved (without fuelling resentments by others towards you)?

_____

_____

What other questions does this chapter raise in your mind? Meditate on the answers.

_____

_____

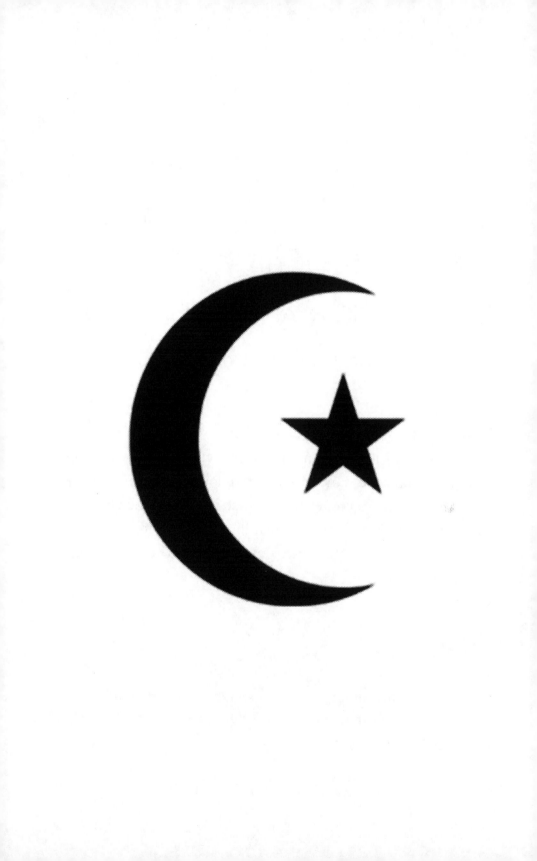

SOW AND REAP

(WHAT GOES AROUND COMES AROUND)

A basic tenet of major religions is that "as you sow, so shall you reap". Reciprocity and consequence of actions is a cornerstone of any social governance system; religion based or otherwise. This tenet is also a cornerstone of justice, underlying all major legal systems, which are, in turn, prerequisites for the social harmony and peaceful coexistence required to sustain the ascent of man.

ISLAM

So, he who has done an atom's weight of good shall see it. And he who has done an atom's weight of evil shall see it. **The Quran-99:7 and 99:8.**[1]

Whoever joins himself (to another) in a good cause shall have a share of it, and whoever joins himself (to another) in an evil cause shall have the responsibility of it. **The Quran, Chapter 4, Verse 85.**[2]

CHRISTIANITY AND JUDAISM

Your eyes shall not pity: life for life, eye for eye, tooth for tooth, hand for hand, foot for foot. **Bible Old Testament, Deuteronomy (19:21), World English Bible (WEB), www. biblegateway.com**

CHRISTIANITY

Remember this: he who sows sparingly will also reap sparingly. He who sows bountifully will also reap bountifully. **Bible, 2 Corinthians(9:6), World English Bible (WEB), www. biblegateway.com**

Don't be deceived. God is not mocked, for whatever a man sows, that he will also reap. **Bible Galatians 6:7, World English Bible (WEB), www.biblegateway.com**

HINDUISM

"Here they say that a person consists of desires. And as is his desire, so is his will. And as is his will, so is his deed; and whatever deed he does, that he will reap." **The Brihadaranyaka Upanishad (IV, 4, ii, 6):): *The Upanishads, Part 2 (SBE15)*, by Max Müller, [1879], at sacred-texts.com**

BUDDHISM

'I am the owner of my actions (kamma), heir to my actions, born of my actions, related through my actions, and have my actions as my arbitrator. Whatever I do, for good or for evil, to that will I fall heir' **AN 5.57 PTS: A iii 71, Upajjhatthana Sutta: Subjects for Contemplation, translated from the Pali by Thanissaro Bhikkhu (1997)**

Whosoever offends a harmless person, One pure and guiltless, Upon that very fool the evil recoils. **Chapter 9:125, Dhammapada Wannapok Translation 1998**

TAOISM

"You cannot find fortune or misfortune on your own, you create them; good will be rewarded with good, and evil with evil, it follows you like a shadow." **The Taoist teaching "Taishangganyingpian",**[3]

CONFUCIANISM

Zi gong (a disciple of Confucius) asked: "Is there any one word that could guide a person throughout life?" The Master replied: "How about 'shu' [reciprocity]: never impose on others what you would not choose for yourself?"—**Confucius, _Analects_ XV.24, tr. David Hinton**

UNIVERSAL HUMAN RIGHTS

Everyone has the right to an effective remedy by the competent national tribunals for acts violating the fundamental rights granted him by the constitution or by law. **Article (8)United Nations Universal Declaration of Human Rights, http:// www.state.gov/j/drl/rls/irf/2008/108544.htm, (This material is in the public domain and may be reprinted without permission; citation of this source is appreciated.)**

SOCIALISM

Do not be cowardly. Be a good friend to the weak, *and love justice.* **Commandment (6) Socialist Ten Commandments, 1912,**[4]

PERSONAL EXPERIENCE

As a child until recently I believed the world and life was not really fair. Why did I have to go through pain? Why were some born into wealth, health, fame and power, while others endured poverty, illness, obscurity and frailty? However, along with spiritual growth, I realized I was basing my conclusion on a partial perception of the world around me. The fact is that with every "blessing" comes a "burden". Injustice tends to be "rewarded" whether sooner or later.

Even though there have been situations where I have experienced bad outcomes resulting from good actions, in almost all cases these outcomes are counter-balanced with good outcomes eventually somehow, as long as I maintain my calm awareness. The perception of good or bad outcomes is not only determined by what happens, but also by my attitude towards life. I spent over half of my life studying to earn multiple qualifications. It is only in the last fraction of my lifespan that I fathomed that it was actually all worthwhile. However, I re-emphasize this was as much to do with the change in my attitude as it was to do with the external outcomes I have experienced around me. My faith in reciprocity, eventual justice, and gratitude for it through calm awareness actually attracts further good outcomes, as well as enabling perception of such outcomes. Rarely does a day go by when my smile is not reciprocated by those I see, or my mistreating others for that matter. If it doesn't happen today, I know it will eventually.

The abuse I was subjected to as a child, whether mental or physical, did not stop with me. I abused others, and I am sure that did not stop with them. The negative feelings of fear, guilt, shame, and remorse were my recompense and probably that of those who abused me. "What goes around comes around". Such a cycle is only likely to be broken with transmuting such negative actions, energy and feelings into positive actions, energy and feelings. While this can be easier said than done, the payoff to me in terms of serenity is profound. After a while, kindness, compassion, love and giving becomes its own reward, without expectation of immediate compensation, or expectation of compensation in like form.

CONCLUDING REMARKS

In pursuing political and economic hegemony and/or control, modern man appears to be oblivious to the consequences of interim actions, and Machiavellian in his approach. We seem to forget the cumulative wisdom that is embedded in our faiths and ideologies. If anything the tenet of reciprocity would be expected to attract constructive rather than destructive behavior, be that toward fellow man or the environment. Somehow, even if justice is not effectively carried out, injustice attracts its own penalty sooner or later.

In a post-colonial or neo-colonial world society we turn a blind eye to the injustices of the past that have led to conflict and turmoil in the present. We bow to power, and justice often takes a back seat or secondary priority. The problem is that injustices left to fester, only lead to growing grievances and resentment, justification of immoral behavior, and ultimately blow up into unmanageable conflicts. The upheaval we see in the world after the colonialism of the nineteenth century, the excesses of the twentieth century, and the financial crisis in the twenty first century, is a manifestation of this "might is right" attitude, obliviousness to the principle of reciprocity, and eventual retribution.

YOUR VIEWS AND REFLECTIONS

CHAPTER 2 (SOW AND REAP)

Do you believe that good and bad actions are ultimately reciprocated? If so, does this happen one for one, or does the reciprocation sometimes come in a different form, or time? Is life generally fair?

_____

Do you generally feel that perception is driven by attitude? Would you say an "Attitude of Gratitude" pays off? Why?

_____

Do you belive that good actions and bad actions are contagious? Does good spread good, and bad spread bad, in the balance? Can good actions become their own reward, and vice versa, i.e. bad actions attract their own penalty, over time? Does individual or collective conscience play a role in this?

_____

Do you believe that in the world we live in a "Might is Right" attitude prevails? If so, how can this attitude be mitigated, or turned around? What can you do about it? And of what value is this to you?

How can past injustices of the powerful be transmuted, if at all? What does your heart and mind say about this?

COMPASSION

(Mi Casa Su Casa)

Closely related to reciprocity, but more encompassing, is the tenet of "do unto others, as you would have them do to you" otherwise known as compassion, or as "loving kindness", or The Golden Rule. Compassion is a sweeping virtue under which many values fall. Would one want to be lied to? Physically or mentally harmed? Raped? Robbed? Conversely, would one wish to be supported and helped in one's hour of need? Would one love to belong? To be praised? To be constructively communicated with? The concept is infinite in application, intuitive, and elementary, yet adopting it with commitment is elusive to many.

ISLAM

And what will make you comprehend what the uphill road is? (It is) the setting free of a slave, Or the giving of food in a day of hunger To an orphan, having relationship, Or to the poor man lying in the dust. Then he is of those who believe and charge one another to show patience, and charge one another to show compassion. **The Quran, Chapter 90, Verses 12-17.**[1]

"O mankind! We created you from a single (pair) of a male and female, and made you into nations and tribes, that ye may know each other (Not that ye may despise each other). Verily the most honored of you in the sight of Allah [God] is (he who is) the most righteous of you. And Allah [God] has full knowledge and is well acquainted (with all things)." **Qur'an, 49:13. Yusuf Ali translation, www.quranexplorer.com**

"A woman who tied a cat will go to Hellfire; she neither fed it, nor allowed it to find food on its own." **The Prophet Mohammed; Narrated By Al-Bukhari**[2]

CHRISTIANITY AND JUDAISM

Because your loving kindness is better than life, my lips shall praise you. **Bible Old Testament, Psalms (63:3), World English Bible (WEB), www.biblegateway.com**

Execute true judgment, and show kindness and compassion every man to his brother. **Bible Old Testament, Zachariah (7:9), World English Bible (WEB),** www.biblegateway.com

CHRISTIANITY

Therefore whatever you desire for men to do to you, you shall also do to them; for this is the law and the prophets. **Bible, Matthew 7:12, World English Bible (WEB),** www. biblegateway.com

JUDAISM

"Do not eat fine bread and give black bread to your servant, do not sleep on cushions and have him sleep on straw." **The Talmud *The Wisdom of the Talmud*, by Ben Zion Bokser, [1951]**[3]

"We are obligated to feed non-Jews residing among us even as we feed Jews; we are obligated to visit their sick even as we visit the Jewish sick; we are obligated to attend to the burial of their dead, even as we attend to the burial of Jewish dead." The rabbis base their demand on the ground that these are *"the ways of peace."* **(Yalkut on Judges 4:1; Gittin 61a.), *The Wisdom of the Talmud*, by Ben Zion Bokser, [1951], at sacred-texts.com**

HINDUISM

Practice compassion, conquering callous, cruel and insensitive feelings toward all beings. **YAMA 7 (of the 10 YAMAS)— Yamas and Niyamas, Courtesy to Himalayan Academy**[4]

BUDDHISM

If anyone, when speaking rightly, were to say, 'A being not subject to delusion has appeared in the world for the benefit and happiness of many, out of sympathy for the world, for the welfare, benefit, and happiness of human and divine beings,' he would rightly be speaking of me. **The Buddha, Bhaya-bherava Sutta: Pali Canon or Tipitaka, translated from the Pali by Thanissaro Bhikkhu, 1998**

TAOISM

Be compassionate and loving! Broadly reach out to bring universal redemption to all! *ChishuYuJue* **(Red Writings And Jade Instructions)The Ten Precepts of Taoism.**[5]

"Regard your neighbor's gain as your gain, and your neighbor's loss as your own loss." **Tai Shang Kan Yin P'ien (Scriptures of Taoism)**[6]

CONFUCIANISM

What is meant by "The making the whole kingdom peaceful and happy depends on the government of his state," this:- When the sovereign behaves to his aged, as the aged should be behaved to, the people become filial; when the sovereign behaves to his elders, as the elders should be behaved to, the people learn brotherly submission; *when the sovereign treats compassionately the young and helpless, the people do the same.* **THE GREAT LEARNING, Confucius, translated by James Legge [1893]**[7]

UNIVERSAL HUMAN RIGHTS

All human beings are born free and equal in dignity and rights. They are endowed with reason and *conscience* and should act towards one another in a *spirit of brotherhood.* Everyone is entitled to all the rights and freedoms set forth in this Declaration, without distinction of any kind, such as race, colour, sex, language, religion, political or other opinion, national or social origin, property, birth or other status. **Article (1) and (2) United Nations Universal Declaration of Human Rights, http://www.state.gov/j/drl/rls/irf/2008/108544.htm, (This material is in the public domain and may be reprinted without permission; citation of this source is appreciated.)**

SOCIALISM

Make every day holy by good and useful deeds and *kindly actions.* **Commandment (3) Socialist Ten Commandments, 1912**[8]

Do not hate or speak evil of any one; do not be revengeful, but stand up for your rights and resist oppression. Do not be cowardly. *Be a good friend to the weak*, and love justice. **Commandment (5)& (6)-Socialist Ten Commandments, 1912**[9]

To fight against all forms of discrimination based on gender, race, ethnic origin, sexual orientation, language, religion, philosophical or political beliefs. **ETHICAL CHARTER *of the* SOCIALIST INTERNATIONAL**[10]

PERSONAL EXPERIENCE

The balsam for my restless spirit has always been to substitute my self-obsession with focus on others. I have not found a better respite from pain. The day I have shown compassion or experienced compassion by others towards me is a day I sense that life has meaning. However, actually succeeding at removing self-seeking behavior is a daily struggle. It has improved for me over time, but it is a long journey, even if definitely worthwhile. Practicing and accepting compassion improves when I engage with others around me, and deteriorates when I isolate. It is fear, greed, disconnectedness and apathy that stand in the way of compassion for others by me. Faith in a higher state of goodness helps me in overcoming these impediments. A wise man once advised me to not only "do for others what you would want them to do for you", but to go beyond that, and "do for others what you would want God to do for you". When he said that I remembered a situation when I was 6-7 year old child, I saw a poor old man sitting across the street from our house looking miserable, and for some reason, that I still do not understand, I went to get him some food from our house, and gave him a kiss on the head. I remember I was actually afraid to go outside to a complete stranger who looked wretched in the street, but for an urge overcame me that was stronger than the fear. The smile I saw on his face never leaves me, and that memory is worth many times more than the bread I gave him, and the kiss on the head. The feeling I have is as if God touches me every time I recollect that situation. However, I have also done things in my life that I am not proud of. There have also been situations when others have shown me compassion. I was saved from a gang of drunk youngsters who attacked me on a train in Europe, as my fellow passengers intervened on my behalf, even though they were clearly afraid of what may happen to them. They also prevented me from doing something foolish in retaliation. Again when I recollect that situation I feel touched by the goodness of the universe. Another situation occurred at a disco dance club, where I was subject to verbal abuse by an intoxicated customer. Again, people came to my defense without being asked. On these occasions, I remember what my father told me as a child about there being "more good in the world than bad", and then life has meaning to me. I believe, at such occasions, that had his observation not been true, we (as a species) would probably not be here today. The fact is that the more compassion I show the more I compassion I get, and the more I get the more I show. It is contagious, and self-perpetuating, as is the opposite.

It is mainly when I am fearful of losing control that I have lost my sense of compassion. This happened when I went into a fight when I was pushed, as a child. It happened when I lost my temper with my own children, or my wife, when I felt that I was losing control of my ability to manage my household "prudently". In most cases, upon reflection, doing so leads to more chaos, not less. My only saving grace then is to humbly apologize, ask for forgiveness for my inordinate response, and make amends.

It is thanks to parents showing me compassion that I have a reservoir of it to show. It is also probably thanks to situations when I was the subject of other people's wrath, as a child, that I carried anger with me to my children. Both pass down from generation to generation, as well as across society at any given point in time.

CONCLUDING REMARKS

If any of the core universal values were to save us by itself, it would be this one, yet most of the world currently operates on the basis of self interest, with an oblivious attitude towards others, and often, even towards our own children, and their own children in future.

Many see this value as a trait of the naïve, the foolish, the idealistic, and the weak, yet all major faiths and ideologies hold that this value is quintessential to the ascent of man. Can they be all wrong? Do they not carry the wisdom of millennia of civilizations? One may notice that the non-theistic governance systems promote conscience, a brotherly spirit and kindly actions, even if compassion isn't explicitly mentioned in the quotes above.

Mercantilism, the industrial revolution, and the nation state, have all rendered us increasingly more focused on me, myself and I, at the individual, the organizational and the societal levels. However, expanding material wealth, without compassion, does not translate into happiness. This is borne out by the Scandinavian experience, where **taxation is highest** for purposes of social welfare, while per capita is still one of the highest in the world, as are life satisfaction indeces.

YOUR VIEWS AND REFLECTIONS

CHAPTER 3 (COMPASSION)

How important do you believe compassion, as a value, is to civilized society? How has modern living influenced practice of this value? Has Compassion made a difference to your life?

Do you believe compassion has an impact on crime, corruption, and malpractice? Why?

How can compassion improve your life, and the life of others around you? Can you think of any initiatives that would engender compassion? Try doing five random acts of kindness, with no expectation of thanks and recompense, then ask yourself and record how it impacts your life for a week, or a day? Try doing the same, for another day, or another week, but ask anyone who wishes to thank you or return the favor, not to do so, but to do the same for three other people, then ask yourself what the impact has been, and record it?

What is the difference between unconditional love and compassion, in your mind? How does that change the way you think about your relationships with your loved ones? Or those who are in need of empathy and compassion around you?

Can compassion go beyond the individual to the institution, or the country? What are the pros and cons of compassion? Which list prevails in the balance?

CONVICTION AND SURRENDER

(I AM A BELIEVER)

Belief in a higher power, or grand design, is another core value, whether that power be the supreme being, universal consciousness, human conscience, or an overriding socio-economic or environmental dynamic. The human being and humanity needs a frame of reference, a coherent dynamic to have faith in, or believe in, or a point of departure that represents a governing and explanatory pattern to fathom a complex existence, and provide guidance and stability amidst uncertainty (and/or chaos, at times). Without this source of relative certainty, enlightenment, and comfort, many would have difficulty with braving the risks associated with the effort required to achieve the ascent of man, or the elevation of self and society to a higher level of existence; a level closer to a preconceived "ideal state". Few would undertake a long and challenging journey into the unknown without a map, compass, or guiding light of some sort. The serenity one acquires when one surrenders to a higher power, or believes in a grand design, inspires and energizes the individual and society to reach for greater heights.

ISLAM

Surely those who believe, and those who are Jews, and the Christians, and the Sabians, whoever believes in Allah [God] and the Last day and does good, they shall have their reward from their Lord, and there is no fear for them, nor shall they grieve. **The Quran, 2:62**[1]

CHRISTIANITY AND JUDAISM

A faithful man is rich with blessings; but one who is eager to be rich will not go unpunished. **Bible Old Testament, The Proverbs (28:20), World English Bible (WEB),** www.biblegateway.com

CHRISTIANITY

Without faith it is impossible to be well pleasing to him, for he who comes to God must believe that he exists, and that he is a rewarder of those who seek him. **Bible, Hebrews 11:6, World English Bible (WEB),** www.biblegateway.com

HINDUISM

"When a devotee has infallible love and devotion for his beloved and Gracious God and he is equally dedicated to his Spiritual Master (who is a God realized Saint), only then that soul (with the Grace of the Saint) perceives, conceives and understands the Divine secrets (and becomes God realized)." **(6/23) Shvetashvatar Upanishad**[2]

BUDDHISM

In this, monks, a monk cultivates Right View . . . Right Concentration that is based on detachment, dispassion, leading to maturity of surrender. **Agantuka Sutta, Tipitaka, translated from the Pali by Maurice O'Connell Walshe, 2009**

TAOISM

Don't criticize or debate the scriptures and teachings! Don't revile or slander the saintly texts! Venerate the Divine Law with all your heart! Always act as if you were face to face with the gods! *ChishuYuJue* **(Red Writings And Jade Instructions) The Ten Precepts of Taoism**[3].

CONFUCIANISM

What Heaven has conferred is called The Nature; an accordance with this nature is called The path of duty; the regulation of this path is called Instruction. The path may not be left for an instant. If it could be left, it would not be the path. **THE DOCTRINE OF THE MEAN, Confucius, translated by James Legge [1893]**[4]

UNIVERSAL HUMAN RIGHTS

THE GENERAL ASSEMBLY proclaims THIS UNIVERSAL DECLARATION OF HUMAN RIGHTS as a common standard of achievement for all peoples and all nations, to the end that every individual and every organ of society, keeping this Declaration constantly in mind, shall strive by teaching and education to promote respect for these rights and freedoms and by progressive measures, national and international, to secure their universal and effective recognition and observance, both among the peoples of Member States themselves and among the peoples of territories under their jurisdiction. **Preamble to the UN Universal Declaration of Human Rights, http://www.state.gov/j/drl/rls/ irf/2008/108544.htm, (This material is in the public domain and may be reprinted without permission; citation of this source is appreciated.)**

SOCIALISM

To carry through progressive politics that favour well-being of individuals, economic expansion, equitable trade, social justice, the protection of the environment in the spirit of sustainable development. To oppose all social and economic politics to the advantage of privileged groups, and promote the creation of a global economic system which will lead to more equitable and fair North-South relations. **ETHICAL CHARTER *of the* SOCIALIST INTERNATIONAL**[5]

Remember that all good things of the earth are produced by labour. Whoever enjoys them without working for them is stealing the bread of the workers. **Commandment (7)-Socialist Ten Commandments, 1912**[6]

PERSONAL EXPERIENCE

I was brought up in a scientifically inclined household, with little conviction in non-tangibly or non-experimentally proven phenomena. Skepticism was my default mode. My unpleasant childhood, and sense of alienation, further reinforced this attitude. I paid the price for this as I grew and life's growing challenges over-burdened me. Anxiety overcame me when I sensed situations were out of control. It was only when I reached a point where my life was about to collapse, and my family was about to give up on me that I submitted to spirituality, and surrendered to the concept of a greater force for good, or universal consciousness that was there to protect and maintain balance. Many of my issues with anxiety, ego and loss of control were mitigated. I was able to see more options available to me to address difficult situations. Spirituality to me meant that I had the conviction that things would eventually turn out for the better as long as I had faith, and surrendered to a greater spirit, being, or universal dynamic. This gave me courage to use my imagination and take risks to address difficulties or find solutions to problems. It also led me to be more modest in my wants, and more focused on my needs, and the needs of the world around me. I would never have had the courage and drive to write this book if I was in my "skeptical" mode. I would not have left a job with a stable flow of income to start a business, or even allow my kids to travel unaccompanied. That is not to say that I do not sometimes inadvertently revert to that mode, however, with faith I am able to muster the will to surrender again. The world and life can be scary to me, and I need to know, in my heart of hearts, that things will work out for the better ultimately, with the help of a universal consciousness. This gives me the drive and confidence to face daunting challenges, look adversity in the face and go on to achieve the "unachievable". Many times, while working on this book project, I was faced with obstacles, and a sense of futility, but I was able to forge along, writing line by line, due to my faith in the effort ultimately fulfilling a purpose, if not for all society, then for a small group, and if not for a small group then for my family, and if not for my family then for myself. Surrendering to a higher consciousness lights my way forward. While mistakes do happen in my life, I take them as learning opportunities, to the extent possible, and avoid using them as an invitation to give up. This is thanks to this faith in a higher being that does not let anything go to waste, and surrendering to it makes the "intolerable" happily "tolerable"!

CONCLUDING REMARKS

While extremes of faith in a single religion or ideology have led to major conflicts in the past, the opposite has not avoided conflict, and attracted peace. Moderate faith, and acceptance of the validity of other faiths and ideologies, in upholding a universal set of core values, should not lead to conflict, but attract the peace of mind required to see the complimentarity, and synergy they can engender in varied contexts.

There may be some who may argue that non-theistic governance systems are not as explicit as faiths in requiring surrender to a higher being. However, if one reflects more closely upon them, one will find that they do engender surrender to the collective will of the people or the proletariat, as the case applies. A higher conscience or higher power almost always manifests itself in collective wisdom.

YOUR VIEWS AND REFLECTIONS

CHAPTER 4 (CONVICTION AND SURENDER)

What faith, and conviction do you have? Is it something that you are willing to surrender to? To risk your life upon? Has it helped you, in times of crisis? Can it be a source of inspiration? Is there a healthy balance between skepticism and faith, that reflects what we know and what we don't know, as individuals, and modern societies? Is the balance out of kilter?

Do you believe in a universal order? Is it a being, a concept, a phenomenon? Do you lose anything by not believing in such an order? If so, what?

How do faith, conviction, surrender, success, and love relate to each other?

Do non-theistic ideologies and governance systems require conviction, and/or faith, in a higher order, or pattern, that leads to the ascent of society? And the individual? Do religious and spiritual orders reform themselves? How?

Is desire to control, an issue for us, as individuals and groups, in modern societies?

GENEROSITY AND GRATITUDE

(Give What You Want to Receive)

Generosity, forgiveness, gratitude and sacrifice are interrelated values, the adoption of which is fundamental to the development of society and the individual. From individual to family to tribe to village to city to nation to humanity to biosphere, connecting to a larger sphere of life through giving and forgiving, is an inherent part of higher consciousness. Gratitude and forgiveness are liberating ideals from a sense of lack or wantonness, that support giving and generosity. Giving and forgiving is the essence of love, and the spiritual glue of society.

ISLAM

Be quick in the race for forgiveness from your Lord and for a Garden whose width is that (of the whole) of the heavens and of the earth, prepared for the righteous,— Those who spend (freely) whether in prosperity or in adversity; who restrain anger and pardon (all) men; for Allah loves those who do good,— **The Qur'an Chapter 3, Verses 133-134, Yusuf Ali translation,** www.quranexplorer.com

And remember! your Lord caused to be declared (publicly): "If ye are grateful, I will add more (favours) unto you; but if ye show ingratitude, truly My punishment is terrible indeed." **The Qur'an, 14:7, Yusuf Ali translation,** www.quranexplorer.com

CHRISTIANITY AND JUDAISM

So are the ways of everyone who is greedy for gain. It takes away the life of its owners. **Bible Old Testament, Proverbs (1:19), World English Bible (WEB),** www.biblegateway.com

The stranger who resides with you shall be to you as the native among you, and you shall love him as yourself, for you were aliens in the land of Egypt; I am the Lord your God. **Bible Old Testament, Leviticus 19:34, New American Standard Bible (NASB),** www.biblegateway.com

Enter His gates with [d]thanksgiving, *And* His courts with praise. Give thanks to Him, bless His name. **Bible Old Testament, Psalms (100:4), New American Standard Bible (NASB),** www.biblegateway.com

CHRISTIANITY

And do not get drunk with wine, for that is dissipation, but be filled with the Spirit. **The Bible, Ephesians 5:18, New American Standard Bible (NASB),** www.biblegateway.com

Let the peace of Christ [m]rule in your hearts, to which [n] indeed you were called in one body; and [o]be thankful. **Bible New Testament, Colossians (3:15), New American Standard Bible (NASB),** www.biblegateway.com

HINDUISM

The riches of the man who gives fully do not run out, but the miser finds no one with sympathy. **Rig Veda, Hymns on Generosity**[1]

BUDDHISM

Generosity, sweet speech, Helpfulness to others, Impartiality to all, as the case demands. These four winning ways make the world go round. **Sigalovada Sutta, Tipitaka, The Discourse to Sigala, The Layperson's Code of Discipline, translated from the Pali by Narada Thera, 1996**

TAOISM

When I see someone unfortunate, I will support him with dignity to recover good fortune. **Scripture on Setting the Will on Wisdom (DZ325). Livia Kohn. Cosmos & Community: The Ethical Dimension of Daoism. Three Pines Press 2004. pp 185-6.**

CONFUCIANISM

Tsze-chang asked Confucius about perfect virtue. Confucius said, "To be able to practice five things everywhere under heaven constitutes perfect virtue." He begged to ask what they were, and was told, "Gravity, generosity of soul, sincerity, earnestness, and kindness." **Confucius Analects (Lun Yu) 17:6**[2]

UNIVERSAL HUMAN RIGHTS

Everyone has the right to seek and to enjoy in other countries asylum from persecution. **Article (14) UN Universal Declaration of Human Values., http://www.state.gov/j/drl/rls/irf/2008/108544.htm, (This material is in the public domain and may be reprinted without permission; citation of this source is appreciated.)**

SOCIALISM

Be as grateful to your teachers as to your parents. Make every day holy by good and useful deeds and kindly actions. Honour good men and women; be courteous to all; bow down to none. Do not hate or speak evil of any one; do not be revengeful. **Commandments (2,3,4)-Socialist Ten Commandments, 1912**[3]

"From each according to his ability, to each according to his needs" **Marx, Karl (1875)."Part I".** *Critique of the Gotha Program*[4]

PERSONAL EXPERIENCE

One longstanding bright spot in my life is generosity. My family were generous with me, and others around us. I have been able to pass that generosity on from time to time. However, earlier in life I would have expectations of recompense for showing generosity. Therefore my gratitude was lacking when I did not get what I considered my fair due, at the very least in the form of recognition, if not otherwise. It is only with spiritual growth that generosity without expectation of any kind of return has been a real blessing. Just the ability to give generates gratitude in me. Perhaps not always, but this is increasingly so. Forgiveness is a form of generosity, in my mind. Again, this is a gift that I have to continually nurture, as I do not always remember that forgiveness actually benefits me as much as the party forgiven. I need to remind myself that resentment is toxic to my own sense of peace. In my case when I am vengeful I am fearful, and when I am fearful my mental capacity to see a multitude of options is restrained, or reduced. I stop seeing solutions, and magnify problems. The peace I feel with forgiveness is akin to the peace I feel with gratitude. They both engender a sense of abundance. Somehow when I am in that mode I sense that good things happen to me without expectation. Can this be just a matter of perception. Perhaps it is partly so, but even logic and rational thinking dictates that when one has a higher capacity to give, forgive, be grateful, and practices it, the more likely that some of that giving, forgiving, and gratitude comes back to one in one form or the other sometimes, if not always, and belatedly if not promptly.

A major example of generosity's influence on me is when I was sent on a scholarship. My gratitude for that generosity shown to me led me to go beyond the call of duty to compensate the party who sent me on the scholarship. This led to a virtuous cycle of giving and forgiving (for the demands made upon me) that catapulted me in my career.

I have found that gratitude is a gift that I need to nurture within me to maximize its blessings, as I live in an age where it is in short supply, and the drive for acquiring "more" is all around me. It is as if I have to train my conscience to remain aware of the blessings I am bestowed with, lest I be sucked into the vortex of insatiable avarice all around me.

CONCLUDING REMARKS

The importance of generosity, as a value, in society is self evident. Social cohesion is built on it. However, in a self centered, individualistic, and impersonal world, it is dying a slow death. Gratitude is in even worse shape, as a practiced value, with demands for "more" in the "here and now", increasing by the day. Each generation takes more for granted, that is provided by technology and exploitation of natural, environmental and other resources. There is a limit to how much the Earth can continue to give in resources, and take back in waste. Our new generation must be raised to be thankful for everything it has, and increasingly try to share with, and give back to, those less fortunate, to reduce the resource depletion rate, and the waste generation rate.

YOUR VIEWS AND REFLECTIONS

CHAPTER 5 (GENEROSITY AND GRATITUDE)

Do you find that you show generosity and forgiveness easily? How often do you expect some form of reciprocity, or recompense? Have you ever given or forgiven anything without expecting something back, in the form of recognition or otherwise? How did that make you feel?

Have you ever tried to "give forward", i.e. give or forgive something, and ask the party you gave or forgave not to thank you, but to do the same for one or more third person? How did that make you feel? Did that feeling last?

_____

Does gratitude come easily to you? Have you ever tried to write a gratitude list before going to bed (5 simple things you are thankful for on a given day)? How does that make you feel? Have you ever tried to consciously foster an "Attitude of Gratitude"? Try it for a week? How do you feel? Does it make you more generous with others?

_____

Can love last without generosity or gratitude? What happens when unconditional love comes into your life?

_____

How is generosity in this day and age? And how is gratitude? Do you believe they are contagious? Do you believe they need to be fostered? What can you do to foster them?

DELAYED GRATIFICATION

(Contentment is a Bottomless Treasure Pot)

Closely related to generosity and gratitude is the capacity for delayed gratification, and achieving satisfaction or contentment with modest gains or small pleasures in the quest for lofty ends. Expecting little yet giving a lot is valued by all religions and ideologies that aim to systemically develop societies, and enhance communal life. This is an especially crucial value with respect to the environment and conservation of resources.

ISLAM

O ye who believe! persevere in patience and constancy: vie in such perseverance; strengthen each other; and fear Allah; that ye may prosper. **The Quran, 3:200, Yusuf Ali translation,** www.quranexplorer.com

Be sure We shall test you with something of fear and hunger, some loss in goods, lives and the fruits (of your toil), but give glad tidings to those who patiently persevere.— **The Quran, 2:155, Yusuf Ali translation,** www.quranexplorer.com

CHRISTIANITY AND JUDAISM

The end of a matter is better than its beginning; Patience of spirit is better than haughtiness of spirit. **The Old Testament, Ecclesiastes 7:8, New American Standard Bible (NASB),** www.biblegateway.com

CHRISTIANITY

So are the ways of everyone who gains by violence;It takes away the life of its possessors. **The Bible, Proverbs—1:19, New American Standard Bible (NASB),** www.biblegateway.com

But the fruit of the Spirit is love, joy, peace, patience, kindness, goodness, faithfulness, gentleness, self-control; against such things there is no law. Now those who belong to Christ Jesus have crucified the flesh with its passions and desires. If we live by the Spirit, let us also walk by the Spirit. Let us not become boastful, challenging one another, envying one another. **The Bible, Galatians 5:22-26, New American Standard Bible (NASB),** www.biblegateway.com

HINDUISM

Practice austerity, serious disciplines, penance and sacrifice.
NIYAMA 10—Tapas, Austerity[1]

BUDDHISM

Conviction is my seed, austerity my rain, discernment my yoke
and plow, conscience my pole, mind my yoke-tie, mindfulness
my plowshare and goad. Guarded in body, guarded in speech,
restrained in terms of belly and food . . . **The Buddha, Kasi
Bharadvaja Sutta: Tipitaka, Kasi Bharadvaja Sutta: To the
Plowing Bharadvaja translated from the Pali by Thanissaro
Bhikkhu 1995**

TAOISM

Do not be lascivious or think depraved thoughts. *Scripture on
Setting the Will on Wisdom* (DZ325). Livia Kohn. *Cosmos &
Community: The Ethical Dimension of Daoism.* **Three Pines
Press 2004. pp 185-6.**

CONFUCIANISM

The Master said, 'The firm, the enduring, the simple, and the modest are near to virtue. **Translation by James Legge, CONFUCIAN ANALECTS**[2]

UNIVERSAL HUMAN RIGHTS

Everyone has duties to the community in which alone the free and full development of his personality is possible. **Article (29) UN Universal Declaration of Human Rights, http://www. state.gov/j/drl/rls/irf/2008/108544.htm, (This material is in the public domain and may be reprinted without permission; citation of this source is appreciated.)**

SOCIALISM

Remember that all good things of the earth are produced by *labour*. Whoever enjoys them without working for them is stealing the bread of the workers. **Commandment (7)-Socialist Ten Commandments, 1912**[3]

PERSONAL EXPERIENCE

Fear of "lack" has always driven my obsessive tendencies; be that lack of recognition, friendship, love, control, wealth, health, etc. Such fears have led me to excesses that I am not proud of. Satisfaction only came to me when I realized that "being satisfied with less" is actually what gives me a sense of "more". Ironic but true. I was a workaholic, but the more success I had the more I wanted, and a lot of the money I made on my job I ended up wasting on my excesses and on doctors' bills later in life. It is only now that I constantly remind and coach myself that accepting less is the only real and sustainable means of achieving satisfaction. I look around me in the life I lead in current society, and most of the messages in media around me drive me to want more, more, and more! It is not easy to counter the deluge, but I have found that meditation, silence, and limiting exposure to media helps to quell the monster of greed that comes alive inside me every now and then.

Delayed gratification was what got me through my education, the nurture of my children, recovery from obsessive tendencies, and the drive to reach out to others, with my experience/s and work.

CONCLUDING REMARKS

The current state in the world runs diametrically opposite to this value, with an incessant and growing need for "instant gratification", be that in terms of material, time, or place. This is, naturally, a socially and environmentally dangerous trend that must be arrested, or even reversed to avoid catastrophe. The history of civilizations has shown time and again that consumptive excesses lead to decay. We see this phenomenon in front of our eyes in comparing recent trends in the West with the East, as the financial crisis leads to the retrenchment of one in contrast to growth in the other.

YOUR VIEWS AND REFLECTIONS

CHAPTER 6 (DELAYED GRATIFICATION)

How do you see the inclination towards delayed gratification developing from generation to generation? Do you feel that our generation seeks instant gratification more than that of our fathers and grand fathers? How about the generation after us? How do technological conveniences and improved standards of living influence that trend?

_____

How important is the link between delayed gratification and gratitude?

_____

Do you believe there is a link between instant gratification, consumption, and resource depletion? Is this sustainable? What can you do to encourage those around you to change this pattern?

_____

How does unconditional love, and compassion, relate to delayed gratification? How about the quest for truth, research, and seeking knowledge?

Do you believe we can save the planet's environment? What do you need to do about it? Can life become easier if we were more restrained in consumption? Can a sense of abundance paradoxically result from delayed gratification?

LABOR AND PERSEVERANCE

(No Pain No Gain)

Common values can only be realized through action. For man and society to ascend to a higher state of consciousness, it is necessary to expend labor collectively, and individually. Compassion and generosity can only be manifested through conscious effort to meet society's needs in the journey of ascent. Each member has a contribution to make, and a role to play, much like the way in which the organs of the body expend effort, each with its own role and competence, contributing towards the human being achieving his/her conscious purpose in life.

ISLAM

O ye who believe! Squander not your wealth among yourselves in vanity, except it be a trade by mutual consent, and kill not one another. Lo! Allah is ever Merciful unto you. **The Holy Quran, 4:29, Pickthall Translation,** www.quranexplorer.com

And when the prayer is ended, then disperse in the land and seek of Allah's bounty, and remember Allah much, that ye may be successful. **The Qur'an 62.10, Pickthall Translation,** www.quranexplorer.com

The Prophet Muhammad (s) said: "It is better for any of you to carry a load of firewood on his own back than to beg from someone else."—[**Agreed Upon] Riyadh-Us-Saleheen, Chapter 59, hadith 540**[1]

JUDAISM AND CHRISTIANITY

Go to the ant, O sluggard, Observe her ways and be wise, Which, having no chief, Officer or ruler, Prepares her food in the summer, And gathers her provision in the harvest. How long will you lie down, O sluggard? When will you arise from your sleep? "A little sleep, a little slumber, A little folding of the hands to [c]rest"—Your poverty will come in like a vagabond, And your need like an armed man. **The Bible, Proverbs 6.6-11, New American Standard Bible (NASB),** www.biblegateway.com

JUDAISM

Great is labor; it confers honor on the laborer. **Judaism. The Talmud, Nedarim 49b, Soncino, page 8**[2]

HINDUISM

He who shirks action does not attain freedom; no one can gain perfection by abstaining from work. Indeed, there is no one who rests even for an instant; every creature is driven to action by his own nature. Those who abstain from action while allowing the mind to dwell on sensual pleasure cannot be called sincere spiritual aspirants. But they excel who control their senses through the mind, using them for selfless service. Fulfill all your duties; action is better than inaction. Even to maintain your body, Arjuna, you are obliged to act. But it is selfish action that imprisons the world. Act selflessly, without any thought of personal profit. **Bhagavad Gita 3.4-3.9**[3]

BUDDHISM

He who says, "It is too hot, too cold, too late!", leaving the waiting work unfinished still, lets pass all opportunities for good, but he who reckons heat and cold as straws and like a man does all that's to be done, he never falls away from happiness. **Buddhism. Digha Nikaya iii.185, Sigalovada Sutta**[4]

TAOISM

Seek neither brilliance nor the void; just think deeply and work hard. **27 precepts of Taoism*Credit is given to Stan**

Rosenthal in his Ch'an Tao Chia: Collected Essays and Lectures by Stan Rosenthal, September 1993[5]

CONFUCIANISM

"That wherein the superior man cannot be equalled is simply this, his work which other men cannot see." (**Doctrine of the Mean, c. xxxiii., v. 2.**), *The Ethics of Confucius*, **by Miles Menander Dawson, [1915], at sacred-texts.com**

UNIVERSAL HUMAN RIGHTS

Everyone has duties to the community in which alone the free and full development of his personality is possible. **Article (29) UN Universal Declaration of Human Rights, http://www. state.gov/j/drl/rls/irf/2008/108544.htm, (This material is in the public domain and may be reprinted without permission; citation of this source is appreciated.)**

SOCIALISM

Remember that all good things of the earth are produced by *labour*. Whoever enjoys them without working for them is stealing the bread of the workers. **Commandment (7)-Socialist Ten Commandments, 1912**[6]

PERSONAL EXPERIENCE

Labor has always been a source of healing for me, but as the sages say, the healing is only effective when the labor is done with the purpose of achieving a greater good. If it is purely selfish, somehow I tend to run out of energy and drive to achieve great things that can make an impact (and cause healing) for me and others. . I was a workaholic, putting in 70 hours (plus), on average in any given week. However, I was doing this mainly for selfish pursuits; money, fame, life's material comforts, and feeding other obsessive tendencies. Now I work many hours less, but achieve more. My focus is on doing the right things, rather than merely doing things right. When I stop doing this for too long (focus on the right things), I despair, and wonder about the efficacy of my existence. Labor expands my presence and enriches it.

CONCLUDING REMARKS

No society in history that has not valued work and labor has had a major mark on the development of humanity. Life cannot be sustained or prosper, by consumption, play and/or worship only. Having said that, work should not be expended for material outcomes alone. In fact, too much of this type of labor comes at the expense of non-remunerated work for self, family and society. Workaholism caused by a single minded focus on material pursuit plagues many societies of this era. Perseverance requires that we balance one type of work with other types, in order to achieve a wholesome existence, even if it means doing with less materially. There are also individuals and societies that tend to live life hedonistically, or at least, want to do so. However, life came to existence through both love and toil, and it is only through toil that it propagates and prospers. Life's very essence is defined by action. It prospers by collective action guided by the enlightened, not the greedy. Recent events, like the Global Financial Crisis, internecine wars, and the so called (oxymoron of the) "War on Terror" do not indicate that our actions are guided by the enlightened, who employ labor and perseverance to help foster life rather than deplete it.

YOUR VIEWS AND REFLECTIONS

CHAPTER 7 (LABOR AND PERSEVERANCE)

How do you see the reverence for labor in our current age? How about perseverance? How does that relate to delayed gratification? How intent are we on seeking quick solutions, that involve little effort, and intense consumption?

How do you feel after you have carried out a task, or project, that requires a lot of effort and patience? Do you find the experience therapeutic? What if the project is done, on a voluntary basis, for charity? How does that feel compared to when one does it for money, or recognition? Which is more lasting and satisfying? Why?

How important has labor and perseverance been to creativity, and to the creative process in your life? Think of the most important work you have produced creatively?

_____

How does perseverance impact on relationships? Do relationships require work? How does labor and perseverance relate to love, and seeking truth?

MEANING TO LIFE

(To Learn, to Love, to Create, and Know Joy)

Life's aim is to propagate itself, in quantity, and in quality, thereby nurturing consciousness. Man is a manifestation of life, and therefore, religions and social governance systems present a path to goodness that realizes Life's aim of expanding consciousness. This means godliness, it means enlightenment, it means connectedness, it means love, it means brotherhood, and union.

ISLAM

Who hath created life and death that He may try you which of you is best in conduct; and He is the Mighty, the Forgiving. **(Quran,67:2), Pickthall Translation,** www.quranexplorer.com

"He brought you forth from the earth and hath made you husband it" (**The Quran, 11:61**). **M.M. Pickthall Translation,** www.quranexplorer.com

"I will create a vice-regent on earth." (**Quran, 2:30**). **Yusuf Ali**

So, when I have made him and have breathed into him of My Spirit, Quran 15:29, **Pickthall Translation,** www. quranexplorer.com

JUDAISM AND CHRISTIANITY

And God blessed them: and God said unto them, Be fruitful, and multiply, and replenish the earth, and subdue it; and have dominion over the fish of the sea, and over the birds of the heavens, and over every living thing that moveth upon the earth. **Genesis 1:28**, **Bible, American Standard Version (ASV),** www.biblegateway.com

And God said, Let us make man in our image, after our likeness: and let them have dominion over the fish of the sea, and over the birds of the heavens, and over the cattle, and over all the earth, and over every creeping thing that creepeth upon the earth. **Genesis 1:26**, **Bible, American Standard Version (ASV),** www.biblegateway.com

CHRISTIANITY

For of him, and through him, and unto him, are all things. To him be the glory for ever. **Romans 11:36**, **Bible, American Standard Version (ASV)**, www.biblegateway.com

HINDUISM

Bright but hidden, the Self dwells in the heart.
Everything that moves, breathes, opens, and closes
Lives in the Self. He is the source of love
And may be known through love but not through thought.
He is the goal of life. Attain this goal!
The shining Self dwells hidden in the heart.
Everything in the cosmos, great and small,
Lives in the Self. He is the source of life,
Truth beyond the transience of this world.
He is the goal of life. Attain this goal! **Hinduism. Mundaka Upanishad 2.2.1-2**[1]

BUDDHISM

For those whose mind is properly cultivated in the Limbs of Perfect Enlightenment, who have no attachment and enjoy in giving up of grasping, and who are free from the corruption, and shine pure in a radiance of light, then attain Nirvana even in this mortal world. **Dhammapada 6:89, Narada Translation 1959**

TAOISM

To know harmony means to be in accord with the eternal.

To be in accord with the eternal means to be enlightened. **Tao TeChing 55, (Wing-tsit Chan translation), chs. 55**

CONFUCIANISM

The Superior man reflects in his person [Heaven's] virtue. **I Ching 35: Progress**[2]

UNIVERSAL HUMAN RIGHTS

All human beings are born free and equal in dignity and rights. They are endowed with reason and conscience and should act towards one another in a spirit of brotherhood. **Article (1) UN Universal Declaration of Human Rights**[3]

SOCIALISM

Make every day holy by good and useful deeds and kindly actions. **Commandment (3)-Socialist Ten Commandments, 1912**[4]

PERSONAL EXPERIENCE

I have spent a large part of my life running away from consciousness, and numbing myself, as I saw everything as an unwanted challenge. I was withering away, running around doing what is expected of me then, numbing myself to face the next day. Spirituality got me to stop and think. It got me to strive to be conscious and more aware of how I can be of most benefit to others and myself in the short journey of life I have left. This requires me to engage with life, empathize, feel, be mindful of the gifts I have, and how they can meet the needs of those around me most effectively. This requires constant calm awareness, faith, love, and a desire to serve. Only then does life have meaning to me.

I owe my existence to the love between my parents. I owe my nurturing to their love of me. I owe my flourishing to love of truth, and the love others have shown me. I owe my sanity to the desire to serve, and seek truth. All these then give my life its meaning.

CONCLUDING REMARKS

Are humanity's actions today consonant with the spirit of the above? Many try, but those who have the upper hand appear to be saying one thing (in harmony with the above), and doing another (in discord with the above). Their actions appear to be saying "we have the means for mass destruction and control, therefore we shall prevail", even if this places at risk the future of the planet, and life on it.

Some say "I think, therefore I am". Others say "We love, therefore we are". Which of them give Life meaning? In this context, Spiritual Love is unconditional. It is essentially Compassion, and selfless service towards attaining a higher state for all of us, for our children, and for their children. At this point, we are not leaving a very good legacy for them. We need to act with enough compassion, enlightenment, and godliness to leave them a better world.

YOUR VIEWS AND REFLECTIONS

CHAPTER 8 (MEANING TO LIFE)

What does Life mean to you? What is its purpose? Do you sometimes feel that you are just going through the motions of living, rather than maximizing your Life's journey, and its value for you, and others?

If you were told that you have one year's worth of life left? What would you wish to have achieved by then? What would you like your legacy to be? Does maximizing contribution to society, through utilizing and building upon your gifts and talents, have a place in that picture? Does love have a place in that picture? Does seeking truth have a place in that picture? What do you need to do to realize that picture?

_____

What does consciousness mean to you? Divinity? Goodness? Godliness? Enlightenment? Brotherhood?

_____

Is Life revered as much as it should be, in our day and age? Is there a tendency to spend our lives focusing on the short term, the fleeting and the material, at the expense of the long term, the long lasting, and the spiritual? Is the balance off kilter, between these two?

_____

What can you do to optimize your Life's journey, and achieve balance? What can you do to encourage others to do so? How can we achieve a higher state of harmony, and synergy, between man, fellow human and nature?

. . .

TRANSCENDENCE AND IMMANENCE

(ALL FOR ONE, AND ONE FOR ALL)

There are often elements of both achieving a higher state through "rising above" or "going beyond" tangible existence (transcendence), and "permeating" or "being one with" universal existence (immanence), in most religious and social governance ideologies.

To a large degree, major religions and social ideologies present an "ideal state" that the individual and society may aspire to. Such an "ideal state" is characterized by all the core universal values, and is conjugal with a state of individual and social harmony, or equilibrium, or even bliss. An aspirational or quasi-utopic end state is essential in modifying crude, primitive, or even destructive social behavior, to become progressively more constructive.

ISLAM

And when My servants question thee concerning Me, then surely I am nigh. **The Quran, 2.186, Pickthall Translation,** www.quranexplorer.com

We verily created man and We know what his soul whispereth to him, and We are nearer to him than his jugular vein. **The Quran, 50:16, Pickthall Translation,** www.quranexplorer.com

CHRISTIANITY AND JUDAISM

He hath showed thee, O man, what is good; and what doth Jehovah require of thee, but to do justly, and to love kindness, and to walk humbly with thy God? **The Old Testament, Micah 6:8, American Standard Version (ASV),** www.biblegateway.com

CHRISTIANITY

And the glory which thou hast given me I have given unto them; that they may be one, even as we are one;**TheBible, John17:22, American Standard Version (ASV),** www.biblegateway.com

But we all, with unveiled face beholding as in a mirror the glory of the Lord, are transformed into the same image from glory to glory, even as from the Lord the Spirit. **The Bible,**

Corinthians 3:18, American Standard Version (ASV), www.biblegateway.com

HINDUISM

He created all this, whatever is here. Having created it, into it, indeed, he entered. Having entered it, he became both the actual and the beyond, the defined and the undefined, both the founded and the unfounded, the intelligent and the unintelligent, the true and the untrue. (**Taittiriya Upanishad 2.6.1**)[1]

BUDDHISM

"Tell them that if they wish to attain that Perfect Enlightenment which Transcends Comparisons they must be resolved in their attitudes. They must be determined to liberate each living being yet they must understand that in reality there are no individual or separate living beings." Subhuti, to be called a Bodhisattva in truth, a Bodhisattva must be completely devoid of any conceptions of separate selfhood." **The Buddha, Vajracchedikā Prajñāpāramitā Sutra, Translated by Edward Conze**

TAOISM

As long as all beings have not attained the Tao, I will not expect to do so myself. *Scripture on Setting the Will on*

Wisdom (DZ325). Livia Kohn. *Cosmos & Community: The Ethical Dimension of Daoism.* **Three Pines Press 2004. pp 185-6.**

CONFUCIANISM

How great is the path proper to the Sage! Like overflowing water, it sends forth and nourishes all things, and rises up to the height of heaven. **Translation by James Legge, CONFUCIAN DOCTRINE OF THE MEAN.**[2]

UNIVERSAL HUMAN RIGHTS

Everyone is entitled to a social and international order in which the rights and freedoms set forth in this Declaration can be fully realized. **Article (28)UN Universal Declaration of Human Rights.**[3]

SOCIALISM

Look forward to the day when all men and women will be free citizens of one community, and live together as equals in peace and righteousness. **Commandment (10)—Socialist Ten Commandments, 1912,**[4]

PERSONAL EXPERIENCE

I must admit that I have not been able to produce anything of consequence without transcending beyond the challenges of the tangible, and the fears such tangibles engender in me. There was a time when my knees would wobble when I had to speak in public. I could only overcome that when I reached a deep conviction that the message I was expressing was much more important than what I looked like in public. If I excel, it is only by connecting, or even uniting, with a higher calling, in the form of the message. If I am to successfully address an important need for those around me I must connect with them, the message, and almost everything else around me. Rationally, this is tantamount to an impossibility, but spiritually it can happen. It is difficult to express in words, yet many of us can feel this sense of transcendence when we sing in a group, or when we overcome a selfish tendency in order to achieve, or contribute to, a team goal, or the collective interest. It is literally an "uplifting" feeling. I personally feel that my life has meaning and purpose in moments such as these, and the obsession with self-preservation becomes a significantly lower priority. Spiritual seekers get a sense of "bliss", and serenity in situations such as these. This makes it more likely that one see the truth, and express it effectively, such that it becomes a unifying force.

CONCLUDING REMARKS

Some may argue that you cannot value both transcendence and immanence, as they are mutually exclusive. Others would disagree, and maintain that you need one to achieve the other. What appears to be common amidst faiths and ideologies is that there is an ideal Oneness that each of them prescribes, be that in the form of a being or an overarching order. What is important for the purposes of this book is that there is a Oneness or ideal end state in which prevail all the core universal values; an end state that entails inter-dependence, or transcending beyond the small self (ego and body), to unite with the Big Self (Universal Spirit).

YOUR VIEWS AND REFLECTIONS

CHAPTER 9 (TRANSENDCENCE AND IMMANENCE)

Have you ever been able to overcome a major challenge, through a drive to achieve the greater good, and place that above your immediate interests or aversions? Did you ever feel empowered by doing what's best for your family, city, country, or the environment, even when that entailed doing something you didn't like, or taking a significant risk, or making a big sacrifice? If so, why? Does that drive relate to transcendence (going beyond), and/or immanence(uniting with/ or becoming part of a bigger thing)?

How do you feel when you transcend the parochial? How do you feel after you have borne sacrifice to answer to a higher calling? Does it attract a sense of peace, tranquility, or even love?

How does it feel when you identify with a wider group? Of people? Of living things? Of entities?

Have you ever sang, with a group of people, or congregation? Have you ever achieved something big, together with a team? What got you, or the group, to succeed?

Have you ever meditated? Sat quiet, in a chair, and just listened to your breath, and what was going on around you, while quieting your thoughts? Try that, preferably in a natural surrounding (e.g. park or garden), and record how you feel? Expand your perception of your surroundings, and ponder on how that relates to transcendence and immanence.

MODERATION AND DETACHMENT

(EVEN NECTAR IS POISON IF TAKEN TO EXCESS)

Balance, moderation, and acceptance of change is another correlated set of virtues that are universally valued in social governance systems, that aim to sustain functional and continuously self-enhancing societies. Extremes in behavior, obsession, rigidity, intolerance, and non-acceptance are patterns that are seen to lead to destructive consequences. Closely related to moderation is detachment (or acceptance). These latter behaviors help avoid a narrow focus and immediate gratification, in favor of a wider perspective, and actions that benefit and complement a grand design, or a larger constituency. Meditation is widely employed as a means of strengthening moderation and detachment (or acceptance), which facilitates sustainability, a broader perspective, synergistic social behavior, and a constructive response to change. The world we live in is subject to many excesses and perpetual change. Acceptance of change (or detachment) is fundamental to healthy adaptation, and spiritual prosperity.

ISLAM

And He it is who causes gardens to grow, [both] trellised and untrellised, and palm trees and crops of different [kinds of] food and olives and pomegranates, similar and dissimilar. Eat of [each of] its fruit when it yields and give its due [zakah] on the day of its harvest. And be not excessive. Indeed, He does not like those who commit excess. **The Qur'an, 6:141, Sahih International translation, Quran.com**

And thus We have made you a medium (just) nation **Qur'an, 2:143.**[1]

CHRISTIANITY AND JUDAISM

It is not good to eat much honey: So for men to search out their own glory is grievous. **The Old Testament, Proverbs 25:27, American Standard Version (ASV),** www.biblegateway.com

Woe unto them that rise up early in the morning, that they may follow strong drink; that tarry late into the night, till wine inflame them! **Bible Old Testament, Isaiah 5:11, American Standard Version (ASV),** www.biblegateway.com

CHRISTIANITY

But the fruit of the Spirit is love, joy, peace, longsuffering, kindness, goodness, faithfulness, meekness, self-control; against such there is no law. **Bible, Galatians 5:22-23, American Standard Version (ASV),** www.biblegateway.com

Be not among winebibbers, Among gluttonous eaters of flesh: For the drunkard and the glutton shall come to poverty; And drowsiness will clothe a man with rags. **Bible, Proverbs 23:20-21, American Standard Version (ASV),** www.biblegateway.com

HINDUISM

Wealth of earth and heaven (prithva and divya) are provided to mankind based on the principle of moderation and selfless work **(Rig Veda 5-68-3 and 4-33-11))**[2]

That soul is not this, not that. It is incomprehensible, for it is not comprehended. It is indestructible, for it is never destroyed. It is unattached, for it does not attach itself. It is unfettered; it does not suffer; it is not injured. *Brihad-Aranyaka Upanishad,* **tr. S. Radhakrishnan, 3:9:26**[3]

BUDDHISM

Hurt none by word or deed. Be consistent in doing well. Be moderate in food. Dwell in solitude, and give yourselves to meditation. This is the advice of the Buddhas. **Chapter 14: 185, Dhammapada, Wagiswara Translation 1912**

Whatever states there are, whether conditioned or unconditioned, of these detachment is reckoned foremost, that is, the subduing of vanity, the elimination of thirst, the removal of reliance, the termination of the round (of rebirths), the destruction of craving, detachment, cessation, Nibbana. Those who have faith in the Dhamma of detachment have faith in the foremost, and for those with faith in the foremost the result will be foremost. **Itivuttaka: The Group of Threes, {Iti 3.41; Iti 87}, translated from the Pali by John D. Ireland, Tipitaka**

TAOISM

Don't take liquor! Moderate your behavior! Regulate and harmonize your energy and inner nature! Don't let your spirit be diminished! Don't commit any of the myriad evils! *Chishu YuJue* (**Red Writings And Jade Instructions) The Ten Precepts of Taoism.**[4]

CONFUCIANISM

While there are no stirrings of pleasure, anger, sorrow, or joy, the mind may be said to be in the state of Equilibrium. When those feelings have been stirred, and they act in their due degree, there ensues what may be called the state of Harmony. **THE DOCTRINE OF THE MEAN, Confucius, translated by James Legge [1893].**[5]

UNIVERSAL HUMAN RIGHTS

Everyone has the right to freedom of thought, conscience and religion; this right includes freedom to change his religion or belief, and freedom, either alone or in community with others and in public or private, to manifest his religion or belief in teaching, practice, worship and observance. **Article (18) UN Universal Declaration of Human Rights.**[6]

SOCIALISM

To carry through progressive politics that favour well-being of individuals, economic expansion, equitable trade, social justice, the protection of the environment in the spirit of sustainable development. To oppose all social and economic politics to the advantage of privileged groups, and promote the creation of a global economic system which will lead to more equitable and fair North-South relations. **ETHICAL CHARTER *of the* SOCIALIST INTERNATIONAL**[7]

To support international action in favour of peace, *tolerance*, dialogue, understanding and cooperation among peoples. To *abstain from using military force* to gain power or to lead a foreign policy, beyond the framework authorised by the relevant international organizations. **ETHICAL CHARTER *of* the SOCIALIST INTERNATIONAL**[8]

PERSONAL EXPERIENCE

Moderation is a virtue that obsessive compulsives like me have a great challenge with. Extremes and excesses helped numb my anxieties. However, I have been able to nurture moderation and detachment with meditation, and spiritual growth, to take the place of excesses, in addressing anxiety. It has been a rocky up-hill climb, but has not been impossible. While I may still indulge in some excesses from time to time, I am conscious of them being so. This helps me with toning down the extremes, and gradually detaching from the hankering that drives me towards them. Detachment is not easy in our current day and age, but when I am conscious about what inordinate attachment does to me, and to those around me, I am able to find the will to devote time and effort to invest in meditation, prayer, and communion with those of like mind. All of these practices help me detach and moderate.

Most, if not all, my excessive tendencies related to my ego, a sense of insecurity, or a sense of lack. Anger, intolerance, resentment and frustration were fed by attachment and obsession, and they, in turn, helped engender further excesses in a vicious downward spiral. Letting go, constantly, helps to reverse that pattern, and fosters the creativity to overcome obstacles, in a healthy constructive fashion. I have found that detaching from preconceived outcomes, or surrendering, is a habit that I need to practice, and remind myself constantly of, many times every day. It is so easy for me to be distracted and pulled towards wanting an increasing mutlitiude of things when I watch modern media, or I am influenced by family, neighbors, friends and colleagues into wanting this or that, that I really may not need. Moderation is a lifestyle choice that has taken me years to cultivate. However, I have noticed that more people in modern society are becoming spiritually inclined, and foster a more moderate and detached mindset. They help keep me motivated to do likewise. I meet with them regularly, to remind myself to stay on track, and be inspired by them.

CONCLUDING REMARKS

Curbing excesses, including excessive attachment to one creed, is at the heart of saving the Earth and Global Society in our current state. Attachment to money, nation, one creed (in contrast to moderation), and influence may be the cause of our downfall as a species, and a planet. The World Wars of the 20th century, global warming, racism, and the clash of cultures are all born of these excesses. All these were or are threats to our very existence.

Meditating on release from these attachments is likely to begin the healing process effectively. We have recently witnessed the excesses of immoral pursuit of profits and money that led to the Global Financial Crisis. We also witnessed the ravages of religious bigotry, nationalist fervor, and geopolitical jockeying in Asia, America and the Middle East. While these types of crises and catastrophes are not new to mankind, the scale and scope of devastation are more horrendous, due to modern technology and armaments. Detachment, moderation and consensus building are required for us to learn from these tragedies.

YOUR VIEWS AND REFLECTIONS

CHAPTER 10 (MODERATION AND DETACHMENT)

How control conscious and obsessed do you feel modern society is becoming? How does this affect your inclinations? Which practices drive you to excess? Which practices help you detach?

How connected do you believe moderation is to saving the environment? What can you do to foster moderation and detachment in your life? Others' lives?

How about peace? Can moderation and detachment help with conflicts? Have you tried solving a problem after practicing meditation, mindfulness, or communion with nature? How did that help in detaching from pre-conceptions and arriving at creative solutions?

How can one balance between ambition, drive, curiosity, and sustainability? Do detachment and creativity have a role?

Can the drive for material progress, and well-being for man and planet, be reconciled? Do moderation and detachment have a role? How about technology? Global society? Can we learn from nature? Are there limits to growth?

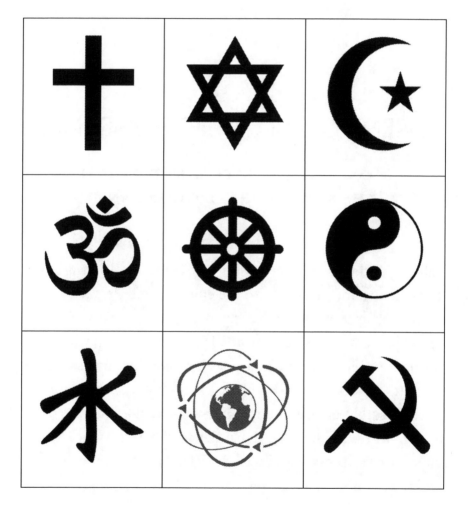

ONENESS AND INTERDEPENDENCE

(IN ONE DROP OF WATER ARE FOUND ALL THE SECRETS OF ALL THE OCEANS)

Interdependence is a cornerstone of communal living, as is constructive integration with the environment. In fact, values such as compassion, and reciprocity, are founded on this prerequisite for civilized society. However, the importance of oneness and interdependence goes beyond human society, the animal kingdom, and the plant kingdom to encompass the biosphere, the earth, and the universe. All major religions have, at their core, cosmic interdependence, wherein typically the concept of oneness goes beyond society, to the environment, and the cosmos, in its entirety.

ISLAM

"We have believed in Allah [God] and what has been revealed to us and what has been revealed to Abraham and Ishmael and Isaac and Jacob and the Descendants and what was given to Moses and Jesus and what was given to the prophets from their Lord. We make no distinction between any of them, and we are Muslims [in submission] to Him [His Will]." **Qur'an, 2:136. Sahih International.**

CHRISTIANITY AND JUDAISM

Have we not all one father? Has not one God created us? Why then are we faithless to one another, profaning the covenant of our ancestors? **The Old Testament, TheBible, Malachi2:10, New Revised Standard Version (NRSV),** www.biblegateway.com

CHRISTIANITY

For in the one Spirit we were all baptized into one body—Jews or Greeks, slaves or free—and we were all made to drink of one Spirit. **The Bible, Corinthians 12:13, New Revised Standard Version (NRSV),** www.biblegateway.com

JUDAISM

"Why did the Creator form all life from a single ancestor?" inquired the Talmud, and the reply is, "that the families of mankind shall not lord one over the other with the claim of being sprung from superior stock . . . that all men, saints and sinners alike, may recognize their common kinship in the collective human family." **The Talmud, (Tosefta Sanhedrin 8:4),** *The Wisdom of the Talmud,* **by Ben Zion Bokser, [1951], at sacred-texts.com**

HINDUISM

LET YOUR AIMS BE COMMON, and your hearts be of one accord, and all of you be of one mind, so you may live well together. **Rig Veda Samhita 10.191**[1]

And when a man sees that the God in himself is the same God in all that is, he hurts not himself by hurting others. Then he goes, indeed, to the highest path.

Bhagavad Gita 13. 27-28. BgM, pg. 101[2]

BUDDHISM

"A monk, mindful, his mind well-released, contemplating the right Dhamma at the right times, on coming to oneness should annihilate darkness" **The Buddha, Sariputta Sutta 4.16, translated from the Pali by Thanissaro Bhikkhu, 1994, Tipitaka**

TAOISM

Maintain a kind heart and do not kill! Have pity for and support all living beings! Be compassionate and loving! Broadly reach out to bring universal redemption to all! *Chishu YuJue* (**Red Writings And Jade Instructions**) **The Ten Precepts of Taoism.**[3]

CONFUCIANISM

Let the states of equilibrium and harmony exist in perfection, and a happy order will prevail throughout heaven and earth, and all things will be nourished and flourish. **THE DOCTRINE OF THE MEAN, Confucius, translated by James Legge [1893].**[4]

UNIVERSAL HUMAN RIGHTS

(1) Everyone has the right to take part in the government of his country, directly or through freely chosen representatives. (2) Everyone has the right of equal access to public service in his country. (3) *The will of the people shall be the basis of the authority of government;* **Article (21) UN Universal Declaration of Human Rights.**[5]

SOCIALISM

To support international action in favour of peace, tolerance, dialogue, understanding and cooperation among peoples. **ETHICAL CHARTER** *of the* **SOCIALIST INTERNATIONAL**[6]

PERSONAL EXPERIENCE

Oneness, when I feel it, is such a source of solace for me. Conceptualizing oneness is not the same as actually feeling it. The breath that I take in, while meditating, connects me to all that is around me. I breathe in the atmosphere, and there is quite little that does not contribute to forming that breath. It is then that I belong. It is then that I connect. It is then that I become part of a much bigger whole, and it becomes part of me. No more estrangement, alienation and apartness is possible at that point. Only then can I be conscious of all that is, and alert or serene or open enough to all the options and possibilities that can take me and all that lives around me to a higher plane of existence.

Interdependence is what I now believe that spirituality and oneness make me conscious of. In my view, all major religions and major social governance systems inspire us to "be the best we can be", as individuals and as societies. That ascendance is only possible with a sense of how interdependent I am, with others in society and with life around me.

Many, if not most, of my issues in life have derived from a sense of disconnection, fear, and in consequence, the desire for complete independence. In a modern individualistic automated world a lot of what is around me encourages this. Oneness through spirituality is my way of counteracting disconnection.

CONCLUDING REMARKS

The essence of the ascent of man is to be conscious of being a part of a larger entity, and inter-dependence is an obvious pre-requisite. The challenge for us now is that the entity we feel Oneness with grows beyond traditional borders.

While technology may lead to our becoming increasingly individualistic and independent, it can also be harnessed to strengthen interdependence. Communication has never been easier, and more far reaching than now thanks to technology. The same applies to travel, and exposure to multiple cultures in one country. All these are channels that can provide insight into how dependent we are on others on the planet, and indeed increase that dependency. This applies as much to products and services rendered by multi-national corporations, as to the environment, or to humanitarian aid at times of catastrophe. Being more conscious of this dependence, increasingly sharing a common set of values, and a common eco-system can help us to empathize with people, other life forms, and the environment in remote places, across the globe. For some, science and technology also helps in clarifying how we are dependent on the cosmos, including our solar system and beyond. When one takes this to its ultimate conclusion it is easy to see how the modern age can potentially help strengthen our sense of Oneness, with the universe. Science tells us that the energy in the universe is manifold more than matter, and that matter can be transformed into energy. This brings us closer to the unifying element that can bring it all together.

YOUR VIEWS AND REFLECTIONS

CHAPTER 11 (ONENESS AND INTERDEPENDENCE)

Do you feel more or less inter-dependent with the world around you, with technology in this modern age? Are you more or less insulated from nature? Society? Family?

Is Oneness more or less important to you having read this far into this book? Why? What can you do to strengthen it, in your life, and the lives of others around you?

How important is a sense of inter-dependence and oneness in mitigating conflicts in the world? Harmony with nature and the environment?

What is the role of schools in enhancing this sense of interdependence? How about travel? Cross cultural exposure? The United Nations and its organs?

_____

Have you ever counted the number of countries you have products from in your kitchen? House? Car? Office? Computer? Also, how many species of animals and plants have contributed to what you have in your kitchen? How important is the Sun, the Sea and Moon to our atmosphere?

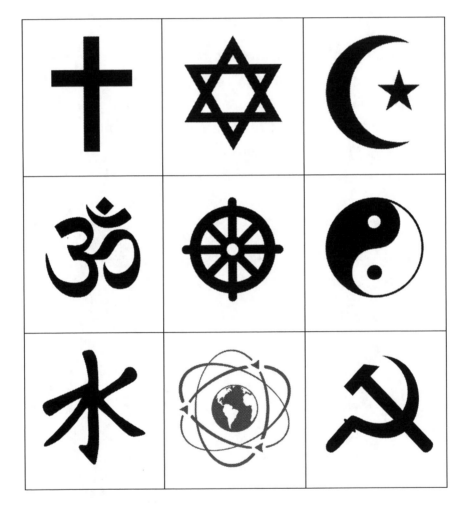

SELFLESSNESS AND EGOLESSNESS

(THROUGH SELFLESS SERVICE, ETERNAL PEACE IS OBTAINED)

When self seeking, and obsession with ego prevail, social cohesiveness pays a price. With inflated egos come fear, greed, arrogance, isolation, blame, guilt, and destructiveness. Social consciousness, compassion, communion, and harmony with the environment require selflessness, and a subdued ego. The ability to triumph over ego, and selfishness, is prescribed by all major religions, spiritual traditions, and social ideologies (or social governance systems). Over the last century or two, man has become obsessed with material accumulation, often at the expense of the interests of wider human society, and the environment. This is the age of "more"; more money, more acquisition, more physical indulgence, more fame, more ego, more control, and many other obsession driven "fixes". The values of balance, moderation, inclusiveness, selflessness, and consciousness (relating to society and environment) do not appear to be prevailing in our current world. If this does not change quickly, we and our children, will pay an unaffordable price. Now is not the time to bicker over petty cultural differences or material acquisition, as life as we know it is at stake.

ISLAM

"(Show) kindness unto parents, and unto near kindred, and orphans, and the needy, and unto the neighbour who is of kin (unto you) and the neighbour who is not of kin, and the fellow-traveller and the wayfarer and (the slaves) whom your right hands possess. Lo! Allah loveth not such as are proud and boastful" **Qur'an,4:36. M.M. Pickthall Translation,** www.quranexplorer.com

CHRISTIANITY AND JUDAISM

Pride goes before destruction, and a haughty spirit before a fall. **Proverbs16:18, The Old Testament, The Bible, New Revised Standard Version (NRSV),** www.biblegateway.com

CHRISTIANITY

But love your enemies, do good, and lend, expecting nothing in return.[e] Your reward will be great, and you will be children of the Most High; for he is kind to the ungrateful and the wicked. **The Bible, Luke 6:35, New Revised Standard Version (NRSV),** www.biblegateway.com

Finally, all of you, have unity of spirit, sympathy, love for one another, a tender heart, and a humble mind. **The Bible, Peter 3:8, New Revised Standard Version (NRSV),** www.biblegateway.com

HINDUISM

"Truth is one, the wise call it by various names." **Rig Veda (1.164.46))**[1]

BUDDHISM

The bliss of a truth-seeking life is attainable for anyone who follows the path of unselfishness. If you cling to your wealth, it is better to throw it away than let it poison your heart. But if you don't cling to it but use it wisely, then you will be a blessing to people. It's not wealth and power that enslave men but the clinging to wealth and power. **Majjhima Nikaya, Sutta Pitaka**[2]

TAOISM

When someone comes to do me harm, I will not harbor thoughts of revenge. **Scripture on Setting the Will on Wisdom (DZ325). Livia Kohn. Cosmos & Community: The Ethical Dimension of Daoism. Three Pines Press 2004. pp 185-6.**

CONFUCIANISM

To show forbearance and gentleness in teaching others; and not to revenge unreasonable conduct:-this is the energy of southern regions, and the good man makes it his study. **THE DOCTRINE OF THE MEAN, Confucius, translated by James Legge [1893].**[3]

UNIVERSAL HUMAN RIGHTS

Everyone has duties to the community in which alone the free and full development of his personality is possible. **Article (29) UN Universal Declaration of Human Rights**[4]

Everyone has the right to freedom of thought, conscience and religion; this right includes freedom to change his religion or belief, and freedom, either alone or in community with others and in public or private, to manifest his religion or belief in teaching, practice, worship and observance. **Article (18) UN Universal Declaration of Human Rights.**[5]

SOCIALISM

Do not hate or speak evil of any one; do not be revengeful, but stand up for your rights and resist oppression. Do not be cowardly. Be a good friend to the weak, and love justice. **Commandments (5) & (6)—Socialist Ten Commandments, 1912,**[6]

To fight against all forms of discrimination based on gender, race, ethnic origin, sexual orientation, language, religion, philosophical or political beliefs. **ETHICAL CHARTER** *of the* **SOCIALIST INTERNATIONAL,**[7]

PERSONAL EXPERIENCE

Self-obsession and egotism have been my bane since childhood. My life has been a continuous struggle against my own self-seeking, and the anxiety that it engenders in me. Not perceiving what was similar between myself and others, as opposed to differences, along with lack of understanding of the needs of others, and their concerns, has caused a lot of anguish for me and them. To be selfless and to deflate ego can be nurtured. I have found that out the hard way. I would add that this practice is contagious. Selflessness spreads, as does selfishness I have also found. To have faith in this is difficult, but experience will show this to be true.

Egotism and selfishness is born of fear and insecurity, and attract more fear, in a vicious cycle, in my experience. They are a product of a sense of lack. Letting go of fear, obsession, possessiveness, and selfishness requires the ability to detach from clinging on to the desire for one thing or the other, and to connect to a much higher calling. I have found that meditation, prayer, healthy food and drink habits, exercise, yoga and voluntary service to those in need all engender the ability to detach. All these activities involve connecting with the world around me and avoid obsessive self-focus. Conducting these activities in groups has further enriched these experiences, in terms of impact on me and on others. To the extent possible, I have involved family as well as friends, in my group activities. I tend to continue to press forward collectively with what they accept, and carry the ball alone, in those activities they don't.

CONCLUDING REMARKS

Individualism, materialism, and instant gratification in our current world help to strengthen ego at the expense of the spiritual connection with society at large, and with other societies and the environment. Spiritual practice is, in essence, about connection. It involves connection with a higher being, the universe, society/ies, nature, our inner selves, and a common calling.

An egocentric or selfish predisposition is predicated on being above, separate, and/or below, people and environment around us, wheras a spiritual disposition is based on equality, connection, and resonance with people and the environment around us. If we, as humanity, are to achieve the ascent of man and society, then this can only be achieved through an egoless spiritual disposition becoming the norm. This should mitigate the manipulation, for power and influence, of societal and religious doctrines by institutions that have political, economic, or exclusionist agendas as their over-riding concerns.

YOUR VIEWS AND REFLECTIONS

CHAPTER 12 (SELFLESSNESS AND EGOLESSNESS)

What does egotism mean to you? Being, right? Superior? Aggressive? Angry? Needy? Lustful? Arrogant? Impulsive? Have you ever felt you were like that? How do you feel after having practiced this attitude time, and again? Guilt? Shame? More egocentric?

_____

Have you ever been selfless and humble? How does that make you feel? Do peaceful, and empathetic come to mind? How important is that to you, and to society? How do you feel when you are compassionate or loving towards someone or something?

_____

How do you see trends in modern society, in respect to these values? What can you do to entrench and perpetuate them? How does one reconcile that with competition and survival of the fittest? Is there a balance to be achieved here? What can you do to restore it, if it is out of kilter?

_____

How does power and the need for control relate to egotism? Are two brains better than one, and three better than two? How do truth seeking and love relate to egotism and selfishness? How about consciousness? Acceptance?

Can heightened attachment to a creed, ethnicity, nationalism, gender, attract egotism?

SHARING THE MESSAGE

(LIFE IS GIVEN TO US, WE EARN IT BY GIVING IT.)

Sharing these core values with our children, our loved ones, and our societies, is in of itself a core value. We must be conscious of how these values are embedded in differing ideologies and religions, and speak to our audiences in a language they understand and are comfortable with. It matters less what the vehicle is than getting to a destination safely. Indeed, at times, obsession with a specific ideology or religion can be destructive to its own core mission. What is the use of administering medicine, when it leads to the patient dying (through being administered in high dosage)? The ultimate, and common goal, is nurturing life, consciousness, and the ascent of man. If implementing a doctrine rigidly leads to harming the common mission, through socio-cultural jockeying, materialistically driven conflict, harming life, degrading the environment, and becoming unconscious or oblivious to other paths (that adopt and maintain these very same core values), which lead to the same ultimate goal, then that would be suicidal. Humanity has established many doctrines to achieve the ascent of man. It has created many languages to explain these means to achieve the ultimate goal. Humanity's challenge in this era is to observe that common core in all of them, and ensure that rigidity in speaking these languages or implementing these doctrines does not lead to these very core values being violated, and the journey to the ultimate goal being threatened or prematurely terminated.

ISLAM

And who is better in speech than one who invites to Allah . **The Quran 41:33, Sahih International translation, Quran.com**

"Convey on my behalf even if it is only one verse" **The Prophet Mohammed, Source: Al-Bukhari**[1]

CHRISTIANITY

"You are the light of the world. A city built on a hill cannot be hid. 15 No one after lighting a lamp puts it under the bushel basket, but on the lampstand, and it gives light to all in the house. 16 In the same way, let your light shine before others, so that they may see your good works and give glory to your Father in heaven. **The Bible, Matthew 5:14-16, New Revised Standard Version (NRSV),** www.biblegateway.com

The gifts he gave were that some would be apostles, some prophets, some evangelists, some pastors and teachers, 12 to equip the saints for the work of ministry, for building up the body of Christ, **The Bible, Ephesians, 4:11-12, New Revised Standard Version (NRSV),** www.biblegateway.com

JUDAISM

"Moses was commanded by the Almighty [at Mount Sinai] to compel all the inhabitants of the world to accept the commandments given to Noah's descendants."(**Maimonides/ Rambam—Mishneh Torah—Sanhedrin Tractate 105b, Hilchos Melachim [The Laws of Kings] Chapter 8, law 10**)[2]

HINDUISM

However, unavoidable adversity overtakes him who does not like to part with Vedic knowledge even when it is asked for. His wishes and hopes, which he would like to gain, are never fulfilled when withholding Vedic knowledge. (**Atharva 12.4.13, 19), Vedic Scripture**[3]

BUDDHISM

"There are these two kinds of sharing: sharing of material things and sharing of the Dhamma. Of the two, this is supreme: sharing of the Dhamma." **Itivuttaka, Tipitaka**

{Iti 4.1; Iti 101}, The Group of Fours translated from the Pali by Thanissaro Bhikkhu, 2001

TAOISM

As long as all beings have not attained the Tao, I will not expect to do so myself. *Scripture on Setting the Will on Wisdom* **(DZ325). Livia Kohn.** *Cosmos & Community: The Ethical Dimension of Daoism.* **Three Pines Press 2004. pp 185-6.**

CONFUCIANISM

The Master observed, "How numerous are the people!" Yu said, "Since they are thus numerous, what more shall be done for them?" "Enrich them, was the reply. "And when they have been enriched, what more shall be done?" The Master said, "Teach them." **Confucianism. Analects 13.**[4]

UNIVERSAL HUMAN RIGHTS

Education shall be directed to the full development of the human personality and to the strengthening of respect for human rights and fundamental freedoms. It shall promote understanding, tolerance and friendship among all nations, racial or religious groups, and shall further the activities of the United Nations for the maintenance of peace. **Article(26)UN Universal Declaration of Human Rights.**[5]

SOCIALISM

We, member parties of the Socialist International, reaffirm our total commitment to the values of equality, freedom, justice, solidarity and peace which are the foundation of democratic socialism. **ETHICAL CHARTER** *of the* **SOCIALIST INTERNATIONAL**[6]

PERSONAL EXPERIENCE

Sharing the message is an experience that I have lived, as a receiver, since childhood. However, its impact upon me was not transformative until I actually lived in a "hell" of my own creation, and until it was conveyed to me, through love, open-mindedness and truth seeking. Prior to that I sensed it was akin to an imposition to achieve conformance. Perhaps this is why a spiritual approach, as opposed to institutionalized religious indoctrination, is seen as more attractive and conducive in this day and age. In my case, it has been the spiritual experience and growth that has shined a light through the layers of rituals and rote learning to the core of religious traditions, and social governance systems. Perhaps the militancy of how God's message/s have been shared in recent history, and the conflict they had engendered is what initially led to my averse attitude. This changed when I experienced love, compassion, and truth seeking, in how the message was conveyed to me through spiritual traditions of late. I have also experienced major positive transformations in physical and emotional health, in me and in social groups around me when we focused on "living" and "sharing" the core values highlighted in this book. Until now, I had been shy in the extent to which I shared these core values, but I don't feel that I would transmute my experience, painful or otherwise, into optimal outcomes without writing this book. I will need to do more, but wish to do so anonymously, as I am conscious of what my ego would do to me and the message if I do this otherwise. You, dear reader, may wish to experiment with living and sharing the core values, to gauge the impact on you and those around you, physically, emotionally, and behaviourally. I have included some exercises and guiding questions, in relation to each value, that may assist you with embarking on this experiment, which is likely to significantly enrich your life journey, as it has mine.

It is thanks to all those who have been generous with sharing their spiritual knowledge that I have come to learn from all major traditions, their respective core values. That is what has inspired me to share what I perceive reverberates across all of them. Sharing what I have learnt is its own reward. I hope that anyone who reads these lines comes to feel as comforted, nay indeed elated, to see that shining common core in all that is humane, and wish to live it and share it.

CONCLUDING REMARKS

While sharing the message of one doctrine may appear to conflict with the sharing of the other's, that is not so when the bearer assigns priority to the core message and universal values. The over-riding considerations are the preservation or nurture of life, compassion, truth and consciousness. If a given path advocates these values then every man or woman, once aware, should be left to his/her conviction.

Possibly the most significant detraction from universal adoption of these core values, would be an exclusionist attitude, or a supremacist approach, requiring a "take it or leave it" response towards a very elaborate doctrinal construct. An incremental inclusive approach is what is likely to be most conducive towards adoption of such a high level framework of values.

YOUR VIEWS AND REFLECTIONS

CHAPTER 13 (SHARING THE MESSAGE)

How have the values above resonated with you? Do they strike you, as being universally core values? If so, do you believe they are worthy of dissemination, as core values? How can one disseminate them?

———————————————————————————————

Is the time right to share these messages? Can each of us, by doing one's bit, contribute to a wave or an awakening? What can you do?

———————————————————————————————

What is the best means of sharing the message? Would it be more effective to focus on any given set of values or religious traditions, or a universal set, or both?

_____

How can we instill these values in the younger generation? Should the Universal Bill of Human Rights be reviewed with input from major religious and spiritual traditions, or social governance systems? How?

_____

How important is this to the well being of future generations? Do we not owe it to them, after the excesses of the twentieth century? How about for the future of our planet?

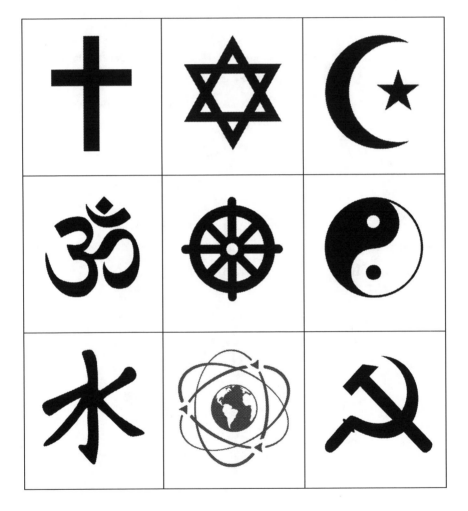

WAY FORWARD

Distilling the essence of the common ground between major faiths and major social governance systems is a necessary, but insufficient endeavor, towards saving humanity from itself (and safeguarding life as we know it). It is suggested that these core values that have held true across time and geography are essential elements of the social code that determines the ascent of societies towards civilization.

The author posits a number of initiatives, in the following, that may expedite the process of re-orientation away from the multiple collision trajectories that were alluded to in the introduction, relating to the environment, culture, socio-economics, and armed conflict. These are proposals for implementation in the short, medium, and long time frames. The ultimate objective is to arrive at a modus vivendi that is sustainable, and a modus operandi that leads to the progressive ascent of man, in terms of consciousness, quality of life, and integration with the environment.

The point of departure must be to agree, at a global forum, such as the UN General Assembly, the UN security council, and/or the G20, upon an inviolable set of core values that all major religious authorities and major proponents of systems of social governance are prepared to observe, such as the one presented in this book. The author does not claim infallibility with respect to what is presented in this book, but is of the conviction that this is a conducive set of core values to begin with, deliberate upon, and possibly amend, if necessary, to arrive at agreement. By so doing, it should be agreed by implication, that any actions or behavior that endangers the aims of the agreed core universal values, in respect to protection of life and environment, must cease. To do so, a body must be set up, with equitable representation (in terms of faith and ideology) that has the means of adjudicating, and enforcing compliance upon member states and bodies. Equitable representation must be based upon number of adherents to a given faith, ideology and/or social governance system, not military or economic power. A human life is a human life regardless of wealth, per capita, ownership of nuclear deterrence, etc.. The means of enforcement must be peaceful, such as through political, social, media based, and if necessary, economic sanctions. Only in situations of highly dangerous, gross and indisputable physical threats to humanity should military force be used, after peaceful means are exhausted. This is a short to medium term measure. In this respect, some may posit that the Universal Declaration of

Human Rights achieves what is being proposed above. While the Universal Declaration encompasses almost all the core values explicitly or implicitly, it does not identify them as a discrete and paramount set of core values that all major faiths and major social governance systems agree upon as being tantamount to a global truth that has been arrived at time and again, across history, culture, and geography.

In the medium to long term, an education and awareness program should be implemented globally to reinforce the importance of the core set of universal values, at the education system level. Along with the primary goal of engendering appreciation, respect and compliance with these values, this measure would have the additional goal/s of attracting respect for humanity's common heritage, and acceptance or affinity towards other major social governance systems and faiths. This must be seen as the very definition of being human or humane. School curricula should cover all major civilizations, how these values led to their prosperity, and how departing from them led to their decay. These curriculum materials should also highlight the impending threats to the environment modern man poses, and the actions or programs being implemented to avert environmental degradation, or even catastrophe, and where such actions may fall short.

Assessments and institutionalized research must be carried out (at both national, and international levels) to determine the impact on the environment, and on global society, if the current trajectories of degradation, *in both*, continue at the current pace. This is important in order to make a determination of what the extent of the threat to life as we know it is, if immediate remedial action and programs are not implemented on the global governance, environmental, socio-economic, cultural, religious, and disarmament fronts. Therefore, the research alluded to here should not be limited to environmental vulnerabilities, but societal, economic and cultural vulnerabilities, as well. The center/s conducting this research should institute a public outreach program to publicize its findings globally.

On a voluntary basis it may be prudent to disseminate the contents of this short book, informally, as well as formally, especially to the young, and those of influence in global affairs to act as an instigator towards agreeing on this set of values as being core and universal, or arriving at an alternate set, if found necessary, by an interfaith and inter-system body as the one proposed above.

SOURCES (By Chapter)

CONSCIOUSNESS CHAPTER SOURCE URL'S

[1] http://www.progressive-muslim.org/Quran-English-Translation.htm

[2] http://www.islamicity.com/forum/printer_friendly_posts.asp?TID=12634

[3] 54/538, http://www.sacred-texts.com/isl/bukhari/bh4/bh4_541.htm

[4] at sacred-texts.com, p. 104

[5] http://www.hindupedia.com/en/Ahimsa_in_Scriptures

[6] http://www.wikipedia.or.ke/index.php?title=Ahimsa

7   Cosmos & Community: The Ethical Dimension of Daoism. Three Pines Press 2004.pp 185-6.

8   http://socialistinternational.org/viewArticle. cfm?ArticleID=24

SOW AND REAP CHAPTER SOURCE URL'S

1   http://www.progressive-muslim.org/Quran-English-Translation.htm

2   http://www.progressive-muslim.org/Quran-English-Translation.htm

3   http://en.minghui.org/emh/articles/2007/2/8/82473p.html

4   http://gdl.cdlr.strath.ac.uk/redclyde/redcly079.htm,

COMPASSION CHAPTER SOURCE URL'S

1   http://www.progressive-muslim.org/Quran-English-Translation.htm

2   http://www.sacred-texts.com/isl/bukhari/bh4/ bh4_541.htm.

3   at sacred-texts.com, p. 105

4   http://veda.wikidot.com/yama-niyama.

5   http://taoism.about.com/od/practices/a/Precepts.htm

6   http://www.freethoughtpedia.com/wiki/Golden_Rule

7   http://www.sacred-texts.com/cfu/conf2.htm

8   http://gdl.cdlr.strath.ac.uk/redclyde/redcly079.htm,

9   http://gdl.cdlr.strath.ac.uk/redclyde/redcly079.htm,

10 http://socialistinternational.org/viewArticle.
    cfm?ArticleID=24

CONVICTION AND SURRENDER CHAPTER SOURCE URL'S

1   http://www.progressive-muslim.org/Quran-English-
    Translation.htm

2   http://www.thevedicfoundation.org/authentic_hinduism/
    bhartiya_scriptures.htm

3   http://taoism.about.com/od/practices/a/Precepts.htm

4   http://www.sacred-texts.com/cfu/conf3.htm

5 http://socialistinternational.org/viewArticle.
   cfm?ArticleID=24

6 http://gdl.cdlr.strath.ac.uk/redclyde/redcly079.htm,

GENEROSITY AND GRATITUDE CHAPTER SOURCE URL'S

1 http://www.indianetzone.com/45/hymns_on_generosity.htm

2 http://classics.mit.edu/Confucius/analects.mb.txt

3 http://gdl.cdlr.strath.ac.uk/redclyde/redcly079.htm,

4 http://www.marxists.org/archive/marx/works/1875/gotha/
   ch01.htm. Retrieved 2008-07-15

DELAYED GRATIFICATION CHAPTER SOURCE URL'S

1 http://www.hinduismtoday.com/modules/smartsection/
   item.php?itemid=4903

2 http://www.sacred-texts.com/cfu/cfu.htm

3 http://gdl.cdlr.strath.ac.uk/redclyde/redcly079.htm,

LABOR AND PERSEVERANCE CHAPTER SOURCE URL'S

1 http://en.wikiquote.org/wiki/Muhammad.

2 http://www.jerusalemlife.com/torahkids/jwquotes.txt

3 http://www.globalcultures.net/asianstudies/Chapter%203-%20
partial.htm

4 http://www.unification.net/ws/theme147.htm#08

5 http://home.insightbb.com/~animal/Tao/Taoist_Precepts.html

6 http://gdl.cdlr.strath.ac.uk/redclyde/redcly079.htm

MEANING TO LIFE CHAPTER SOURCE URL'S

1 http://www.unification.net/ws/theme020.htm

2 http://www.unification.net/ws/theme020.htm

3 http://www.ohchr.org/EN/UDHR/Pages/Language.
aspx?LangID=eng

4 http://gdl.cdlr.strath.ac.uk/redclyde/redcly079.htm,

TRANSCENDENCE AND IMMANENCE CHAPTER SOURCE URL'S

1   http://en.wikipedia.org/wiki/Ishvara

2   http://www.sacred-texts.com/cfu/cfu.htm

3   http://www.ohchr.org/EN/UDHR/Pages/Language.aspx?LangID=eng

4   http://gdl.cdlr.strath.ac.uk/redclyde/redcly079.htm,

MODERATION AND DETACHMENT CHAPTER SOURCE URL'S

1   http://www.progressive-muslim.org/Quran-English-Translation.htm

2   http://www.sabhlokcity.com/metaphysics/chapter9.html

3   http://www.san.beck.org/GPJ3a-UpanishadsYoga.html

4   http://taoism.about.com/od/practices/a/Precepts.htm

5   http://www.sacred-texts.com/cfu/cfu.htm

6   http://www.ohchr.org/EN/UDHR/Pages/Language.aspx?LangID=eng

[7] http://socialistinternational.org/viewArticle. cfm?ArticleID=24

[8] http://socialistinternational.org/viewArticle. cfm?ArticleID=24

ONENESS AND INTERDEPENDENCE CHAPTER SOURCE URL'S

[1] http://www.unification.net/ws/theme029.htm

[2] http://theoracleinstitute.org/quotes-on-truth

[3] http://taoism.about.com/od/practices/a/Precepts.htm

[4] http://www.sacred-texts.com/cfu/cfu.htm

[5] http://www.ohchr.org/EN/UDHR/Pages/Language. aspx?LangID=eng

[6] http://www.socialistinternational.org/viewArticle. cfm?ArticleID=24

SELFLESSNESS AND EGOLESSNESS

[1] http://www.hinduwisdom.info/introduction_to_hinduism.htm

2 http://www.beliefnet.com/Faiths/Buddhism/Buddhist-Quotes.aspx?p=754

3 http://www.sacred-texts.com/cfu/cfu.htm

4 http://www.ohchr.org/EN/UDHR/Pages/Language.aspx?LangID=eng

5 http://www.ohchr.org/EN/UDHR/Pages/Language.aspx?LangID=eng

6 http://gdl.cdlr.strath.ac.uk/redclyde/redcly079.htm,

7 http://socialistinternational.org/viewArticle.cfm?ArticleID=24

SHARING THE MESSAGE

1 http://www.islamweb.net/emainpage/articles/92752/index.php?page=showfatwa&Option=FatwaId&Id=103070

2 http://www.noachide.org.uk/html/history.html.

3 http://www.sacred-texts.com/cfu/conf1.htm and http://classics.mit.edu/Confucius/analects.3.3.html

4 http://www.stephen-knapp.com/vedas_say_they_must_be_shared_with_everyone.htm

5 http://www.ohchr.org/EN/UDHR/Pages/Language.aspx?LangID=eng

6 http://www.socialistinternational.org/viewArticle.cfm?ArticleID=24